THE NATIVE UNIVERSE AND MUSEUMS
IN THE TWENTY-FIRST CENTURY

NMAI EDITIONS

THE NATIVE UNIVERSE AND MUSEUMS IN THE TWENTY-FIRST CENTURY

The Significance of the National Museum of the American Indian

With a Foreword by

W. RICHARD WEST, JR.

Founding Director of the National Museum of the American Indian,
Smithsonian Institution

National Museum of the American Indian
Smithsonian Institution
Washington, D.C., and New York
2005

Library of Congress Cataloging-in-Publication Data

The Native universe and museums in the twenty-first century : the significance of the National Museum of the American Indian.
    p. cm.
Papers presented at the opening international symposium of the National Museum of the American Indian held Sept. 20, 2004. Includes bibliographical references and index.
ISBN 1-933565-00-4
I. National Museum of the American Indian (U.S.)—Congresses. 2. Indians of North America—Museums—Congresses. 3. Ethnological museums and collections—Congresses. I. National Museum of the American Indian (U.S.)
E56.N37 2005
970.004'97'0074753—dc22
2005022319

Manufactured in the United States of America
The paper used in this publication meets the minimum requirements of the American National Standard for Permanence of Paper for Printed Library Materials Z39.48-1984.

National Museum of the American Indian
Project Director: Terence Winch, Head of Publications
Symposium Coordinator: Nicole Oxendine Poersch (Lumbee)
Designer: Steve Bell
Editors: Mark Hirsch, Amy Pickworth
Photo Research: Mia Ritzenberg

The National Museum of the American Indian, Smithsonian Institution, is dedicated to working in collaboration with the indigenous peoples of the Americas to foster and protect Native cultures throughout the Western Hemisphere. The museum's publishing program seeks to augment awareness of Native American beliefs and lifeways, and to educate the public about the history and significance of Native cultures.

For information about the Smithsonian's National Museum of the American Indian, visit the NMAI website at www.AmericanIndian.si.edu. To support the museum by becoming a member, call 1-800-242-NMAI (6624), or email aimember@nmai.si.edu.

Title Page: The east-facing main entrance to the National Museum of the American Indian at dawn. Photo © 2004 Judy Davis/Hoachlander Davis Photography

TABLE OF CONTENTS

A cascade flows over a boulder known as a Grandfather Rock at the northwestern end of the
National Museum of the American Indian's water feature. Photo by Maxwell MacKenzie © 2005.

W. RICHARD WEST, JR.

(Southern Cheyenne and member of the Cheyenne and Arapaho Tribes of Oklahoma)
Founding Director, National Museum of the American Indian

CULTURAL FUTURES

AT THE NATIONAL MUSEUM OF THE AMERICAN INDIAN, we are engaged in a continuous discussion about what we are doing, what we need to do, and how to do these things better. This kind of discourse is common to any organization, but our analyses are not based on number-crunching. For guidance and assistance we look to the public we serve—to both Native and non-Native visitors to the George Gustav Heye Center in New York City and our museum in Washington on the National Mall, to curators and conservators, to historians and anthropologists, to educators and schoolchildren, to artists and performers, and, most importantly, to Native peoples throughout the Western Hemisphere. While all of these conversations are important, some are informal and impromptu in nature; others are planned and much anticipated. The Opening International Symposium of the National Museum of the American Indian belongs to the latter variety. This conversation, held September 20, 2004, on the very eve of the opening of the Mall Museum, was critical to the process of examining our mission, revealing what that mission requires us to do, and doing those things better than we may have in the past.

When I became the director of the National Museum of the American Indian in June of 1990—which seems, on the one hand, almost like yesterday, and on the other hand, as though it were an eternity ago—I looked abroad for inspiration as to how we might fulfill the museum's mission as we had defined it. I found a great deal of good work being done in countries such as Australia, New Zealand, and Canada, where the indigenous populations were working with cultural institutions to participate, in a real and meaningful way, in the process of determining how their cultures should be represented. I wanted to tap a number of the people at the center of these efforts, as we began work on creating our own museum. Papers by those people and others, highly esteemed colleagues all of them, are included in this book.

The Opening International Symposium posed the question: *What is the significance of the National Museum of the American Indian?* There are many ways to go about answering that deceptively simple question. One way is to study it through the lens of museology, from the viewpoint of how museums do their business. In that way, I think that the National Museum of the American Indian has attempted, in a consistent and systematic way, to go about the representation and interpretation of Native peoples in a somewhat different fashion than the typical museum. I should emphasize that it is not as though we invented the concept—we listened to what Native people themselves were saying they wanted, and talked to some of the most innovative people in the museum world today. This concept had already been applied in other museums regarding Native peoples right here in the United States. But I think the National Museum of the American Indian marks the first time that, on this scale and at this magnitude, this kind of representation has been attempted.

Exactly what do I mean by this kind of representation? Well, I would say that the heart of the mission of the National Museum of the American Indian is two-fold. First of all, we are emphatic about the notion that Native cultures and peoples exist across a long continuum—one that has great depth and a great past, one that antedates the arrival of Europeans in this hemisphere by thousands of years, and one that encompasses the emergence of significant and complex societies and civilizations. And we absolutely need to realize this, because it means that Native peoples, as the originating elements of civilization and cultures, are the original source of the national cultural heritage of every citizen of the Western Hemisphere, whether Native or non-Native.

Looking to the present, there are some thirty-five to forty million indigenous people alive, if not always well, throughout the Americas. Native peoples are not some kind of ethnographic remnant waiting to be pushed off the stage of history or to disappear quietly. As Native people, we have fought very hard to stay here, and we will stay here, and we will insist on some kind of cultural future in this hemisphere.

The second aspect of the National Museum of the American Indian, which sits at the core of our thinking, is the invocation of Native or first-person voices in the interpretation and representation of Native peoples. I emphasize that this statement is not intended to denigrate existing systems of knowledge that have been used in the past to represent and interpret Native peoples. Anthropology, archaeology, art history, history—all are systems of knowledge that have had great value in the interpretation and representation of Native peoples, our lives, our ideas, our cultures, and our cultural patrimony. We are simply acknowledging that included in the conversation about Native peoples should be Native peoples themselves.

We have tried to make the National Museum of the American Indian a different kind of cultural destination than most museums. In the course of building mutually participatory relationships with Native communities, what became clear to me was that a *museum*, in the future and very best sense of the word, is not limited to a role as an educational source of entertainment. While it certainly is that, it can also become an actual civic space. I believe that in this country, where civic spaces—whether in the form of the church, the town forum, or the town hall—are in a state of decline or at least a state of atrophy, creating spaces of a civic nature that serve as *fora* to address issues of the society at large is a very worthy aspiration. That is not the way museums are seen by many people, but it happens to be the way that I see them, and I know that it is the way Native people see them. If the National Museum of the American Indian is going to be valuable to contemporary Native peoples, we must somehow link what we talk about inside the museum to larger issues that sit in the world outside. It is that process of exchange and bilateralism that transforms a building from being a museum in the conventional sense of the word to being a true civic space that becomes something far larger in concept, in practice, and in meaning.

What is the significance of the National Museum of the American Indian? There are many answers to this question, most of which will only be revealed to us over time. As we continue to work toward becoming a vital civic space for Native communities throughout the Americas, we consider the challenges presented to us by our esteemed colleagues on the day of our Opening Symposium and in the resulting papers in this book. We are deeply indebted to them for their invaluable insights, guidance, and companionship on our journey.

NMAI Founding Director W. Richard West, Jr., with the museum's Native cultural interpreters, 2005. Front row, from left: Renee Gokey (Eastern Shawnee/Sac and Fox), Jared King (Diné), Shirley Cloud-Lane (Diné/Southern Ute), W. Richard West, Jr., (Southern Cheyenne/Arapaho), Lorisa Qumawunu (Hopi), Edwin Schupman (Muscogee), Jose Montano (Aymara). Back row, from left: Benjamin Norman (Pamunkey), Sharyl Pahe (Diné/San Carlos Apache), Phillip Hillaire (Lummi). Photo by Genevieve Simermeyer (Osage). © NMAI.

Visitors participating in the Winter Round Dance in the Potomac area of the National Museum of the American Indian, 2005. Photo by Katherine Fogden (Mohawk). © NMAI.

ELAINE HEUMANN GURIAN

Senior Museum Consultant
Founding Deputy Director for Public Program Planning, National Museum of the American Indian

Coming Full Circle

Coming full circle means coming together with the ones who were here before,
to be one with the spirit and the mind.
—J. Van Pelt, 2002[1]

Having worked for W. Richard West, Jr., as the first deputy director for Public Program Planning at the National Museum of the American Indian (NMAI), I want to attest that in addition to his obvious grace and elegance, which we admire (and also joke about), his commitment to his people is unstinting and his moral center is unswerving. He is a man who is steadfast in friendship, brave enough to make tough decisions, willing to follow grand visions, and comfortable with the messy approximations of real life. It was a pleasure to work for him, it remains a pleasure to call him "friend," and I know that I speak for all when I say, Rick, you richly deserve all the accolades that you have and will continue to receive. No one else could have birthed this museum, and we are all profoundly grateful to you.

Our audience today includes museum colleagues from all over the world who have participated in the creation of their own museums and who, therefore, recognize best the struggle, dreams, and daily hard work of those among us whose work this achievement represents. So, will the members of the NMAI team, both past and present, staff and consultants, advisors, board members, builders and designers, and anyone else who visualizes themselves as part of this creation, please rise to receive the ovation you richly deserve. Your peers, who understand what you went through, wish to recognize you and your achievement.

Welcome

I wish to acknowledge the original inhabitants of this land. That sentence is the traditional first passage uttered at all public gatherings in Australia (as you will hear again from our Australian speakers) and seems just right as a welcome today. The original inhabitants of this land were Native people. If we are referring to the Chesapeake region, we must recognize the Piscataway, Nanticoke, and Powhatan peoples. If we are referring to this continent, many tribes of indigenous people lived here, all special and amazingly diverse, and that too should be celebrated. And if we are metaphorically referring to the peopling of this national museum, then the citizens and guests who begin arriving today are this building's original inhabitants, for this place was built for everyone. I do indeed wish to acknowledge them all.

This day marks the end of the museum's seemingly interminable planning phase, and the beginning of its "being" phase. On this day before the public opening, the museum will be a private reality, seen by the privileged few. But tomorrow and forever more, this museum on the Mall will welcome all.

For those of our future audience who will visit only the Mall, the museum will feel like the one and only National Museum of the American Indian. In reality the Mall museum is the last of four entities, the other three having opened during the previous twelve years. For those who collectively created the National Museum of the American Indian, all four elements constitute the whole and each would not be considered complete without the other three. The opening of the Mall museum represents a "coming full circle," as Pablita Abeyta, a longtime staff member, sculptor, and member of the Navajo Nation, said to me yesterday.

The first element of the NMAI to open was the George Gustav Heye Center in New York, reminding us all that the original Museum of the

American Indian originated in that great city. The second was the Cultural Resources Center (CRC) in Suitland, Maryland. Many Native people would say that the CRC is the soul of the museum because their tribal treasures are housed there, and Indian people are encouraged to visit their tribal patrimony privately and traditionally within its walls.

Perhaps the largest and most salient component of the NMAI is not a building at all; it is the "the fourth museum," which includes all of the outreach programs, the website, books and recordings, and, most especially, the work of the Community Services Department, the museum office that closely interacts with Native communities around the hemisphere. From the earliest time, the NMAI made a commitment, based on consultations, to work directly with Indian tribes in their individual homelands on issues of the tribes' choice, and to create a mutual relationship that would unite knowledge and material held in many places. Members of different communities can attest to this invisible, but vital, interplay between themselves and the staff of the NMAI for the benefit of their own tribe and their own people.

The Role of the Elder

To place this symposium in context one must talk about mentors, both personal and historic. The NMAI is a groundbreaking museum. The opening of the National Museum of the American Indian on the National Mall integrates the American Indian's story, tangibly told from their own perspective, into the patriotic national pilgrimage to Washington, D.C. Visitors to this new museum, who are used to the curatorial voice of mostly white academicians, will be surprised and perhaps a little disconcerted by this new and unfamiliar approach. Indians have officially arrived in public Washington. As Jette Sandahl writes:

> The opening of the National Museum of the American Indian obviously signifies a readiness and even a need for the inclusion of the stories of Native Americans in the official history writing of the United States as a nation. Politically, it is remarkable for the open recognition and acknowledgement of the disrup-

tive, abusive, and unsettled character of this history. And it is a sign of the strength of Native American communities to have brought about this kind of answerability.

As George MacDonald points out, the NMAI joins other national museums of indigenous history to mark a "shift toward the integration of New World history into the history of mankind."

While the NMAI is in some ways unique, it is not without precedents. The museum builds upon models set by others, and its director, Rick West, has had the comfort of the company of other museum leaders whose personal bravery was instrumental in establishing relevant and pioneering museums, exhibitions, and policies.

Rick chose to open the Mall museum celebration by offering this symposium. It establishes the NMAI on the Mall as reflective and maturely self-aware behind its more obvious public face. I would suggest that this symposium also marks Rick's very personal thanks to his museum guides and mentors, because when Rick began as director, he knew a lot about Native Americans, but precious little about museums. In order to break the mold, he needed to know what the mold looked like and who his mold-breaking forebears were. You will hear from some of his guides today.

I am not a historian, and so I cannot acknowledge all the important guides of the past. Nor can I cite all of the early anthropologists, art historians, and collectors who spoke against prevailing practices but failed to secure the changes in museums they wished for. The transformation of institutional voice from academics to the direct voice of indigenous creators and their descendants has been a long time coming. Those who helped in that transformation deserve our thanks.[2]

I learned from George Horse Capture about the power of the elders and the obligations one has toward them. As he told me many times, "When your elders call you home, you go." It has become clear to me that the term "elder" is not about age alone. It is about leadership. The Maori word *Mana* may also be apt here because it applies to humans and objects alike and is about the emanation of power coming from a moral center.

The speakers chosen by Rick represent a collection of "elders," regardless of their age or cultural background, who actively participated (and continue to participate) in changing the dynamic of practice in the world of museums. They did so at great personal risk, often with their jobs on the line, and all of them with courage in the face of displeasure from the powerful. They are iconoclasts, all, and much respected by their more timid colleagues. The people you will hear today were changed by a vision of inclusion, and when looking at the museum institution, each found it wanting. Each person then created or worked on projects that altered the mold.

Having worked at the NMAI in the earliest consultation phase, I wish to thank my guides and elders. My mentors are the deserving recipients of any credit I have received because I was brash, impetuous, self-assured, and unruly when I entered this work. I was eager to establish a bridge between the Smithsonian establishment, from which I was transferred, and the American Indian community. Some Native American mentors were assigned to chaperone me and help me understand what I was listening to. And each of my minders gave up a considerable amount of social capital to be seen with me, because each of them had status in their own community, while I had none.

Each Native co-leader stood at these consultations and said publicly that they had faith in this project. They believed it would happen and that they would personally insist that their commitments would be realized. The people who stood at those early consultations and vouched, occasionally reluctantly, for me, were Dave Warren, Rina Swentzell, Suzan Shown Harjo, Pablita Abeyta, Arthur Amiotte, the late Lloyd Kiva New, Rick Hill, and George Horse Capture. George made a personal decision to watch, goad, and persuade from inside the NMAI staff. I thank you all for taking such a chance, and I hope you will see that the reality of the NMAI has been faithfully achieved through your aspirations.

The Museum and Its Changing Relationship to the Object

Over the last two decades, marginalized people worldwide, especially indigenous peoples, have been responsible for instigating profound and fundamental changes in the practice of museums through their individual and collective exhortations. Indigenous activists, holding fundamentally differ-ent world views from those operating museums, clamored for a different re-lationship between themselves and the museums that housed objects cre-ated by their ancestors. Their arguments rested on their deep belief in the power dwelling within and surrounding the material.

Objects were not to be considered "dead," which was, and is, the prevail-ing assumption of museum collections. Jette Sandahl, in describing these fundamental differences, writes:

> Gently, the Native American communities and now the National Museum of the American Indian insist on ignoring, avoiding, evading, or transcending the dichotomous hierarchies of West-ern Civilization. They refute the most basic of binary hierarchies of mind over matter in the continuous respect for objects as "liv-ing entities," containing "living spirits" and "conscious beings" with physical, emotional, and spiritual needs of their own. And for them it is part of the responsibility of museums to reflect these needs and provide the opportunities and conditions suit-able for "the cultural integrity of the object."

Bernice Murphy, in reflecting on the acceptance (in the 1980s) of Australia Aboriginal art within mainstream art museums, suggests:

> [A]rt images are readily understood as partial but also special kinds of subjectively encoded phenomena. They are not pre-sumed to "represent" persons, communities, or lifeways in a merely referential or ethnographically normative sense. This does not mean, however, any lack of interest in deepening layers of knowledge (social, communal, scientific, even psychological knowl-edge) as a supplement to experience.

The Results of the First Peoples' Demands on Museums

Indian agitation resulted in changed national laws and museum policies. Most especially a changed power relationship has arisen between museums and the descendants of the makers of their collections. However, First Peoples needed allies within the museum establishment. George MacDonald, placing new museums in the context of current post-colonial and post-modern perspectives, finds these museums to be

> more complex, more multifaceted, and more inclusive than the previous single-perspective model based on Western values of rationalism and colonialism. This newer perspective promotes more intercultural understanding, more intimacy and sharing of histories, and more mutual trust and respect than was possible in earlier museum presentations, which polarized indigenous and colonial perspectives.

Many First Peoples felt that museums had failed them. From my point of view they were and are right in their assertions. We still have much work to do; the negotiation between Native peoples and museums is an evolving one. Yet changes have been made. A partial listing would include new formulations of ownership, reburial of human remains, repatriation of secret and sacred objects, ceremonial access, change in collections-care procedures and in the control, promulgation, or withholding of intellectual content.

These papers can be read as a continuous history with the dialectic left in. For example, Jette Sandahl reminds us that other marginalized people, whether their condition is based on culture, gender, sexual orientation, and conquest, have a stake in the outcome of these museum changes.

Des Griffin leads us through the political transformation in Australia. We learn that museums can effect changes even before there is widespread acceptance within the political mainstream, and in so doing, can influence public debate.

Rick West asserts that the new NMAI is "an actual civic space," and wishes museums to take on that role even more strongly and intentionally than before.

Cheryll Sotheran points out that the changes affect much more than content. Her paper leads us to understand how thorough changes must be to implement a commitment to biculturalism.

Bernice Murphy tells us how Aboriginal Australians, previously excluded from art museums and relegated to cultural presentations only, became accepted and integrated into the art museum structure. This history has repercussions for all artists of many cultures who were segregated into specific institutions. This integration remains an uneasy relationship today, between traditional art forms wherever they are found and art museums, and between producers from specific cultural groups and mainstream art museums.

As Rick Hill, a member of the original team of advisors, a former staff person at NMAI, an art curator, and a member of the Tuscarora Nation, points out, museums have not changed enough, even while he acknowledges things have changed. He cautions that "museums may have a stifling effect on the vitality of indigenous life because of the need to minimize the expression of the culture to fit the needs of the museum."

Finally, Amar Galla argues that integration is essential in other forums as well as museums and that we cannot rest until many different kinds of assemblies respect many different viewpoints.

One of the beneficial unexpected consequences of these new relationships was the establishment of individualized negotiations between specific museum directors and tribal leaders, which produced solutions that were specific to the situation. Stultifying precedent was not to become the overarching criteria for solutions. It was this advisory process between Native stakeholders of goodwill and open-minded museum directors that developed an arena of approximation, accommodation, negotiation, and invention without apology. It was the elevation of the messy middle.

While Native peoples worldwide, but most especially in Canada, New Zealand, and Australia (followed by the United States), were demanding changes, indigenous people were joined by a few museum leaders who were primarily white. As Des Griffin writes, "In these contested and sometimes unsafe space-times, many museums are light-years ahead of political leadership."

Our panel includes some of the leaders whose sympathy and personal bravery was such that they were willing to join, negotiate with minority people, and together create new forms of administration, ways of working, and new kinds of policy. Often this required taking stands against their colleagues. These museum leaders played the role of important bridge builders. As this history is told, they also need to be recognized. The speakers today represent some of the museum leaders who worked on the side of indigenous colleagues to change prevailing practices and instigate new ways of doing things.

Des Griffin

Des Griffin is the former director of the Australian Museum and is the originator with others of the policy paper that changed the relationship between indigenous people and museums in Australia. This policy became the model for other countries to follow. Des writes about the changing policy within Australian museums and its consequences internationally. Des is acknowledged worldwide as one of the agents of change in the work between museums and indigenous people.

Dame Cheryll Sotheran

Dame Cheryll Sotheran was the chief executive of the Museum of New Zealand Te Papa Tongarewa, when it radically rethought itself and opened in a new building on the Wharf in Wellington, New Zealand. Te Papa is acknowledged as one of the great museums in the world, and for her participation, her country awarded her with its highest honor, the title "Dame."

As part of its thoroughgoing reassessment, Te Papa was determined to become bicultural in every way. The management was reorganized into a duality with two chief executives "in all critical areas of policy and practice of the museum, not solely in aspects of the museum that involved . . . Maori knowledge and protocols." The Maori chief executive, *kaihautu*, during Cheryll's tenure was the carver, Cliff Whiting, and I wish to recognize that the current *kaihautu*, Te Taru White, is with us today. We welcome your presence here.

Cheryll's paper describes what it means to be the chief executive (and one of two leaders) in an institution that takes its commitment to a bicultural reality seriously, and in which two people must forge a relationship and create governing protocols where none have existed before.

Jette Sandahl

Jette Sandahl is the director of the Museum of World Cultures in Gothenburg, Sweden, which opened on December 29, 2004. Jette was the founding director of the Women's Museum in Denmark, a radical institution in that country, and went on to be the head of exhibitions for the National Museum of Denmark. During her tenure, the museum began implementing its commitment to multicultural power-sharing in a way not seen before in Scandinavia. The Museum of World Cultures is even more radically attempting to enable a formerly homogeneous country to understand and embrace all the cultures of its new immigrants and more. The museum has already proven to be an outstanding public success.

Jette's paper explores the effect European colonization has had upon the ways museums and indigenous peoples are viewed, and how the new museology represented by the opening of the NMAI can help to redress past wrongs for all marginalized peoples.

Amareswar Galla

Amar Galla was born into a hill tribe in India called Chenchu, lives in Australia, and works on behalf of indigenous peoples worldwide. His focus has not been place-specific; rather, he works and writes about community issues and museums. He speaks from the intriguing perspective of one minority culture working with others in a setting not his own.

George MacDonald

George MacDonald became director of the Canadian National Museum, Museum of Civilization, in Hull, Canada, after a very long career as an anthropologist. At the Museum of Civilization, he led his staff from their rather traditional role into one that utilized the power of technology. Through his dauntless understanding of technology, George got the rest of us over a fearful hump—showing us that technology was not an alien force but a power that should be part of our armamentarium. George went on to become the director of the Museum of Victoria in Melbourne, Australia, and has recently retired as director of the Burke Museum in the state of Washington. He is now returning full circle to his beloved Canada. His paper allows us to understand the process that created the groundbreaking introduction of the First People's Hall into the Canadian National Museum.

Bernice Murphy

Bernice Murphy is the former director of the Museum of Contemporary Art in Sydney and a noted curator of art in Australia. In her paper she traces the transformation of Western views of Aboriginal art from anthropological evidence to its acceptance as an important genre within the fine art community. Bernice played a significant role in that change. She continues to be devoted to museums, working at the highest levels of the International Council of Museums (ICOM) on policy changes between all nations and their museums.

Rick Hill

Rick Hill is a member of the Beaver Clan of the Tuscarora Nation. Among his many positions, he has been assistant director for Public Programs for the National Museum of the American Indian. He left NMAI because he was called home to his reservation by his elders. He is one the foremost American Indian art and exhibition curators, having helped with the opening exhibitions at the Heye Center and many others. Rick Hill makes it amply clear that there is much work yet to do. His humor and his skepticism serve good purpose. We are indebted to him for keeping us focused and forthright.

Closing

One can argue that any single museum—and especially museums created by marginalized people—can act as metaphors for all. Indigenous efforts to transform the very foundational notions of the museum—calling for museums to become welcoming civic spaces and asserting that objects by themselves, devoid of their context and their story, must not be the focus of our work—have changed museums forever.

However, there are even more underlying reasons to be grateful to First Peoples. When dealing with museums, they have demonstrated a willingness to live within approximation, negotiation, humor, multiple voices, and change. And in the face of longstanding disappointment, they have remembered and retained their core values. They have rewarded and recognized conscientious Native and non-Indian people who have joined them in their struggle. Today you will hear from some of the people who made this change possible.

Tomorrow, the NMAI, having come full circle, starts around again, with the Mall museum beginning its long journey as an evolving, changing institution—full of adaptability and notions of multiple solutions, full of cultures that reach to the past and adapt and live equally in the future, full of the big picture and exquisite detail, and full of spaces for conversation, celebration, study, and contemplation. The museum will be full of welcome for all. It will integrate sight with sound, place objects into context, and blur the borders between the inside space and the land that surrounds it.

I am not an indigenous person but I, too, belong to an ancient tribe: the tribe of Israel. In our calendar, this week marks "the days of awe," our holiest week. By reflecting, atoning, and praying, we hope to be "written" into the book of life for the coming year. How fitting it is that I can help open this museum, as awesome as it is, during my tribe's "days of awe." At such a celebration, it is customary for Jews to recite a special prayer of joy and of rejoicing (the Shehecheyanu). It goes as follows:

Barukh attah Adonai eloheinu melekh ha-olam,
she-hecheyanu v'ki-yemanu v'higianu lazeman hazeh.

Translated it says,

Praised are You, Lord our God, Ruler of the Universe, who has kept us alive, sustained us, and brought us to this special time.

NOTES

1. Foreword to D.C. Stapp and M.S. Burney, eds. *Tribal Cultural Resource Management: The Full Circle to Stewardship,* 4th ed. (Walnut Creek, CA: Alta Mira Press, 2002), ix-xii.

2. Knowing that this is a partial list with additional names omitted out of ignorance, I wish to recognize Suzan Shown Harjo, Daniel Monroe, and Martin Sullivan for their work on the creation of *Native American Graves Protection and Repatriation Act,* Public Law 101-601, 101st Congress, November 16, 1990, 104 Stat. 3048; Tom Hill and Trudy Nicks for their work on *Turning the Page: Forging New Partnerships Between Museums and First Peoples: Task Force Report on Museums and First Peoples,* 2nd ed. (Ottawa: Assembly of First Nations and Canadian Museum Association, 1992); Cliff Whiting, the Maori carver of distinction who was the first *kaihautu* of Te Papa, the National Museum of New Zealand; Christopher Anderson, the former director of the Museum of South Australia, who worked alongside Des Griffin to create "Previous Possessions, New Obligations," a policy adopted by the Council of Australian Museum Associations in December 1991, published in *Previous Possessions, New Obligations* (Adelaide: Museum of South Australia, 1993); and Dawn Casey, an Aboriginal woman, who was the director during the construction, development, and opening of the National Museum of Australia in 2001.

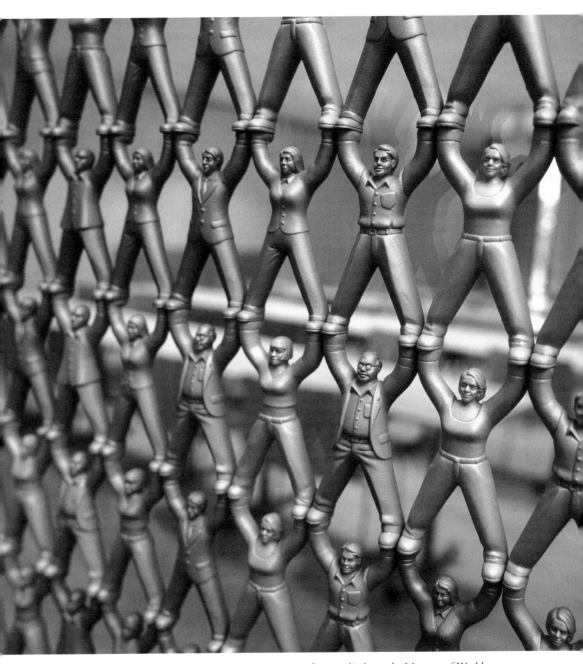

Screen, by Do Ho Suh, is the only permanent piece of art on display at the Museum of World Culture, Gothenburg, Sweden. The museum opened to the public on December 29, 2004. Photo by Åke Fredriksson.

JETTE SANDAHL

Director, Museum of World Culture, Gothenburg, Sweden

LIVING ENTITIES

ACROSS THE GLOBE, THE OPENING OF THE National Museum of the American Indian on the National Mall stands as a milestone event, with wide-ranging symbolic value and multilayered museological and political meaning.

Historically, museums have been among the most central institutions of nation building, in which new trends of national self-definition, of national identity, and national demarcations are played out. Our period is no different. New national museums are new official national self-portraits.

The opening of the National Museum of the American Indian signifies a readiness and even a need for the inclusion of the stories of Native Americans in the official history writing of the United States as a nation. Politically, it is remarkable for the open recognition and acknowledgment of the disruptive, abusive, and unsettled character of this history. And it is a sign of the strength of Native American communities to have brought about this kind of answerability.

In museological terms, certain key concepts are already distinctly associated with the formation of the National Museum of the American Indian. These include the principles of peoples' rights of self-representation; of consultations and shared authority between the museum and representatives for the (original) producers and owners of the collections as well as other potential stakeholders; and the visions of a cultural institution as a site of empowerment for subjugated groups and as a site of reconciliation between warring and opposing peoples. The political and museological movement, out of which the National Museum of the American Indian grew, encompassed new museum institutions in other parts of the world. Some of these were in direct communication; some were connected only through the priorities and synchronicity of the times. Some are national; some are defined through specific terms of ethnicity, gender, or class. Across these differences many museums of the 1980s and 1990s share the intent of giving voice to those whose points of view have been muted as part of the specific politics of power. For all of us involved in breaking new museum ground in this period, our purpose and efforts have been given authority by the dignity and credibility of the Native Americans in the forming and shaping of their museums.

The National Museum of the American Indian suggests and advocates metaphysics and cosmologies that deal in ethical terms with the creation and order of the universe and the spiritual relationship between mankind and the natural world. Gently, the Native American communities and now the National Museum of the American Indian insist on ignoring, avoiding, evading, or transcending the dichotomous hierarchies of Western Civilization. They refute the most basic of binary hierarchies of mind over matter in the continuous respect for objects as "living entities,"[1] containing "living spirits" and "conscious beings" with physical, emotional, and spiritual needs of their own. And for them it is part of the responsibility of museums to reflect these needs and provide the opportunities and conditions suitable for "the cultural integrity of the object."

The National Museum of the American Indian encourages us as museum professionals to let go of the idea of ownership of collections, and to acknowledge instead the honor and responsibility of being their collective stewards. It allows for the various realities of different peoples and persuades us to trust in different versions of history—in history not as "a single, definitive, immutable work, but as a collection of subjective tellings by different authors with different points of view." It shows us the changing forms in which cultures survive, and the resilience of peoples adapting to new conditions while they keep their cultures alive. It shows us that there is no single lifestyle befitting living cultures in the multifaceted, continuously changing, contemporary context. It promises that we can have it both ways: We can remain loyal to our "tribal"—in whichever way this concept applies to our context—traditions and ways, and still demand participation and influence in the processes of mainstream society.

The museums of the American Indians fill us with excitement and hope, not only for their insistence on having their histories presented and represented, but even more so for their consistent affirmation of their own cultures that continuously represent alternative worldviews and alternative forms of spirituality. The courage of the Native American communities in claiming and asserting precisely those values, practices, and beliefs that have been the basis for their exclusion and persecution stands as a steady source of inspiration to the rest of the professional community.

Genocidal Fury and Rational Violence

As a European museum professional, I find it necessary to dwell on the atrocities emanating from that continent, and on the specific logic of what has been called "the excluded, yet constitutive other" that I believe we still find hard to escape in contemporary museums. Flashing back to the time of European colonization of the Americas, we uncover a Renaissance Europe steeped in violence and genocidal fury, where the brutality against people of the Americas links up with centuries of war against Muslim people in Europe, Africa, and Asia, with the imaginary crimes of the witch persecutions, with the accelerating enslavement of African peoples, and finally, with a new set of scientific paradigms.

The expansion from the European continent and the transition from medieval to modern times seem to depend on the figure of "the other" as a projection ground—a figure of "otherness" made up of everything European man was trying to leave behind in his feudal past and in his relationship to nature as a living being.

A new concept of rationality and a new white male character structure was formed through the subjugation of women and peoples of other regions and cultures and through the suppression of their traditions, moral practices, and cultural expressions. Throughout the next centuries, up to our time, again and again, "otherness" is defined relative to this particular form of rationality.[2] Descriptions of the devastation of the Indies[3] read with painful familiarity: the meticulousness of the terror; the ingenious methods of torture maximizing both pain and humiliation; the patterns of gender and the manifestations of power and dominion through sexual aggression; the destruction of the women through the children, the men through the women; the religious overtones and undercurrents; the disbelieving victims who think it must all be a mistake; the discredited, mistrusted eyewitness accounts.

Philosophies of nature were changing radically in Europe in the sixteenth and seventeenth centuries. The so-called scientific revolution advocated a much more interventionist approach to the study of nature and to the use of natural resources than had been believed appropriate within medieval traditions. Philosophies of rights of the emerging bourgeois society were ambiguous, advocating principles of equal rights while simultaneously defining the exclusion of large populations, at home and at large.

Civilization and Its Dispossessed

Native Americans were forced to obey the superiority and rights of rule of the conquerors—or "all harm and damage, the deaths and losses which shall accrue, are their own fault."[4] The perceived embeddedness with nature of the indigenous populations of the Americas became—as was the perceived embeddedness of women with the natural forms of love, sex, and marriage[5]—the basis for their exclusion from civilization and from their status as full citizens.[6]

The absence in Native American cultures of individual possessions, private property, and legal regulations of ownership were contrary to the European philosophical system of "possessive individualism"[7] of the late seventeenth and eighteenth centuries. A puzzled Christopher Columbus described the people who "never refuse anything which they possess, if it be asked of them; on the contrary they invite to share it."[8] Likewise, the practices of hunting and gathering, rather than cultivating the vast and shared territories, were adverse to the emerging view of nature as a thing to be conquered and mastered, controlled, formed, and shaped. Gradually, the collective use of vast shared territories was identified as the "uncultivated waste of America"[9] and was seen as a crime against both "God and Nature," through which Native Americans were understood to have forfeited or squandered the ownership of their lands.

In the twisted turn of fate and history, cultivation of land became a norm that allowed the accusation that Indians were "usurping for the purposes of barbarism, the fertile lands, the products of mines, the broad valleys and wooded mountain slopes, which organized society regards as magazines of those forces which civilization requires for its maintenance and development."[10] This juxtaposition of barbarism to civilization implied specific character traits of primitivity and lack of reason that prohibited Native Americans' participation in the processes of modern society. They had to be taught the European work ethic and the art of civilization, and they had to be protected against themselves in the "dangerous transition from savage to civilized life."[11] The exclusion was argued in terms of character traits, or what would now be called psychological terms, as the presence or absence of rationality or reason.

The Past as a Foreign Country

Increasingly, these mechanisms of inclusion and exclusion became cloaked in the scientific terminologies of evolutionary theory. Museums in particular became showcases where the color-coded and gender-coded hierarchies of the evolutionary point of view found their material substantiation. New displays, for instance, of the collections of the National Museum of Denmark from the 1840s were organized through the classification of the objects, cultures, and peoples into a three-age evolutionary system of distinct and successive periods that became paradigmatic within museums and within archaeology.

In a succession of twenty-two rooms, the exhibitions showed "the wild people, who ordinarily do not themselves make metal, and who must therefore be considered on a lower level," followed by "the nations that do work with metals, but cannot yet be considered as having by themselves developed literature," and finally "those nations that have all the abovementioned conditions for culture. . . . Obviously descent, climate, and other factors play a part, but it is surprising to what extent even distant nations are like each other in tools and other means they use, when they stand on the same stage of culture."[12]

Once this system of hierarchy in the development of cultures from the "wild peoples" and "those of lower cultural stages" to "those in transition to higher cultures" was in place, real interest could shift to the "information that can be harvested from the ethnographic collections regarding our own prehistory." The specific steps and stages of the evolutionary ladder now become firmly identified with various stages of the European past, with the more ancient periods corresponding to ever-lower cultures of foreign continents. Europeans had come to see their own past as a foreign country. And museums excluded foreign cultures from a historic context by demoting them to a pre-history that leads up to but is not a part of civilization.

Aboriginal Populations of the Mind

Evolutionary thinking is characterized by movement, by change, by succession. In the thinking of nineteenth-century philosophy and sciences, primitivity and backwardness became unmistakably associated with the peoples outside Europe. Primitivity also increasingly became something one would outgrow—as an individual and as a society. The new science of psychoanalysis in the early twentieth century merged ontogenetic and phylogenetic developments. It fused the primitivity of the so-called wild people with the primitivity observable in children.

In normal human development, primitivity would be retained only in this terra incognita of the psyche that had now been discovered: the unconscious. "The content of the unconscious is like an aboriginal population (*Urbevölkerung*) of the mind,"[13] Freud said in one context, and he consistently compared his methods for uncovering this content, layer by layer, to those of archaeology, reaching ever older and more primitive civilizations buried under the younger.

Through a very free interpretation—should I say free association?—of anthropological, childhood, and patient observation, a normative model of psychological health was created, in which attaining a mature personality requires leaving behind the specific modes of each developmental stage. What is left behind and outgrown sums up centuries of descriptions of peoples outside Western civilization—and of women: emotional and intellectual forms associated with immediacy of desire, with wishful thinking and belief in the power of thought to alter the external world; with superstition and animist belief in magic and the omnipotence of gods; with simplicity and concreteness, incapability of negations, mutual contradictions, and logical operations.

As opposed to naturally given rights and static principles of feudal society, movement and transitions were distinguishing qualities of the new modern period. In the philosophies of rights and history of the nineteenth century, there is perpetual unrest and changeovers of ascendancy among individuals, groups, and societies. Likewise, while in psychoanalytic principle maturity and rationality are attainable for all human beings, the dynamic nature of the psychoanalytic system is also threatening, in that primitivity is something into which everyone can backslide, revert, or regress if they are not careful.

Enfranchisement demanded of Native Americans that they leave behind the reservation and their traditional practices to adopt the "customs and habits of civilization" and thus gain the rationality required for status as citizens. In psychoanalytic interpretations through the twentieth century, individuality and maturity correspondingly involve a differentiation and separation from—and a repudiation of—the undivided oneness and emersion with nature and with the maternal.[14]

Emotional Epistemologies

Late in the twentieth century, various voices of otherness started opposing these general psychological norms for their bias towards the male, urban, white, Western. They started claiming some of the excluded values, but most importantly, they seriously questioned whether an inclusive "both-and" was not often truer and more appropriate than the oppositional "either-or" of binary thinking.

Individuation and character formation were reinterpreted as cultural constructs rather than as biological facts, placing the norms of the twentieth century in the specific—and anything but universal—patterns of urban Western environments, with the highly polarized family life of domestic motherhood and distant fatherhood. Rejecting the binary mold and its radical opposition between individuality and communality, between dependency and separateness, we emphasized responsiveness and mutual recognition in the processes of individuation. We looked to the positive factors of emulation, continuity, and sameness for the healthy formation of identity and personality. Maturity thus became rooted in connectivity and intersubjectivity, where unity and at-oneness are embraced and do not bear the psychological stigmata of primitivity or regression into prehistoric backwardness.

A similar and related critique was voiced within epistemology against the scientific methods of knowledge formation. Moreover, this critique within epistemology started interacting with and merging with the political movements of the time—the civil rights movement, the student movement, the women's movement, and the movement to protect the environment.

The platform, for instance, for the Women's Museum of Denmark in 1982 consciously and actively opposed the traditional dichotomies of scholarly methods. We tried to establish new standards and a new vocabulary. We "did not believe in an objectivity defined as the opposite of the subjective." We did not believe that things were more truthful or more objective the less they seemed related to one's subjective reality. Subjectivity for the Women's Museum is a unity of emotions and intellect, of feeling and thinking, and the museum sought working methods that consciously integrated and made use of this subjectivity. Empathy, compassion, solidarity, and awareness rather than denial, containment rather than splitting off emotions, are thought to lead to "a fuller intellectual clarity, to transparency rather than scholarly blind spots."[15]

In contemporary philosophy of science, these intentions have been labeled a dynamic rather than a static pursuit of knowledge and objectivity.

It recognizes that the subject and object are not just the same; they need to be disentangled to reflect both the independence and the connectivity between the two terms.[16]

Dialogues of Dilemmas: A Museum of World Cultures

Here are some kaleidoscopic snapshots of another new museum I am now helping to create.

The Museum of World Culture in Sweden is working on the same agenda as the National Museum of the American Indian, namely, transcending colonialist and imperialist legacies, of going behind or beyond evolutionary positions and interpretations, and of developing paradigmatic and epistemological shifts that can explore and facilitate a range of other perspectives and world views. The museum holds an ethnographic collection, gathered—or hunted—with the passions of the quest for knowledge, but marred and disfigured by the asymmetrical power relationships of colonialism and undertows of European supremacy and careless appropriation.

New collecting is essential, or the museum will become a mausoleum of nineteenth and twentieth-century evolutionary discourse—but collecting is done with some trepidation. There is, with these colonial collections in Europe, no easy fusion between the museum subject and object. Even with the most careful recruiting policies and most personal of research strategies, the distances of time and place, the gulfs of wealth and perspective, are hard to bridge, intellectually and emotionally. Only through global partnerships, collaboration, and a sharing of knowledge and collections so radical and profound that they are still hard for us to imagine[17] will it be possible to document and represent living cultures and give different peoples, across time and place, credence as historical subjects.

I see the Museum of World Culture as part of a larger government effort to reorient and reinterpret Sweden as a nation within a context of accelerated globalization and migration, of increased connectivity and dependence across the world, but also of increased possibilities for difference and individuality. Geographic areas, nationality, or ethnicity are basic analytic parameters for a museum of world cultures, but one inevitably reflected these days through the powerful lenses of accelerated globalization. World cultures also include communities created through age, education, and gender, as well as shared lifestyles, shared enemies, shared poverty, shared diseases, and shared tastes in food, in fashion, and in bed. The professional and popular partnerships, networks, and experts of the museum reflect this range and diversity.

Welcoming the plurality of multiple voices, the museum is aiming for the highest international standards of performances, but it is also actively seeking out and inviting in representatives of the most vulnerable, most muted, and excluded otherness—the dreamlike elusiveness and the spiteful rejection that thrives beyond even the fringes of society.

Similar to the National Museum of the American Indian, the Museum of World Culture is meant to be prospective as much as retrospective. We aim to create a museum within the terms of mutuality and connectivity, through the methods of interpersonal resources and skills, empathy, understanding, and solidarity. We experiment with trusting our intuition and risk focusing on individual voices to avoid the tired clichés of official history; we trail personal friendships and follow family links in the diasporas around the world. We record the oral stories as told, as we know that the spoken word comes to the muted and silenced voices before the written.

In research and exhibitions, the emotional realms serve as much as structuring principles as do chronology, materials, and scientific disciplines. We do not allow deviation from rationality to be defined as irrationality, nor do we allow opposition to realism to be defined as unrealistic. We feel comfortable within the oxymorons of magic realism.

Protecting, to the best of our abilities, the collections for eternity, we subscribe to the idea of the permanence of a river, accepting that truth or interpretation are never identical but always fluid, changeable, and new. The museum will thus have no permanent galleries but will show changing special exhibitions. Some of these will originate from our collections; some take their themes from contemporary issues; but all of them reflect the past as seen from the present as much as the present is interpreted on the basis of the past.

In all of them we mix media; we blur the boundaries between different methods and scientific divisions. Historic and ethnographic collections co-exist with contemporary art; art is challenged by its continuum into documentaries and into works originally intended as personal, therapeutic, or political. The exhibition medium is stretched to the breaking point through its integration of dance, theater, and music.

We know enough about the inertia of institutional power to set ourselves up willingly to lose control. We know that the museum is never the sole judge of the right presentation of subjugation, celebration, oppression, and dignity. We initiate processes of empowerment in which we know that success will unsettle institutional patterns and precarious balances. We warily invite the tension and the rage of the powerless against the complacency of an institution and a country that smugly thought we had it made.

Interesting dynamics are set free in societies when those who share the predicament of otherness relative to the dominant powers discover mutual identification.[18] We wonder if the many voices of otherness can come together in one museum. The diversity we seek to articulate is less one of easy harmony than one of recognition of conflicts. We search for the place where difference and disagreement are accepted—even celebrated—and are not coded into binary oppositions and hierarchies of inferiority and backwardness, superiority, dominance, and supremacy, a place where the violence of evolutionary rationalism is suspended and dialogue may begin.

A film clip in the National Museum of the American Indian shows a Native American insisting that his life "is not an ancient fantasy." I have come to the same position the long way around, through the intertwined histories of scientific paradigms, museum displays, and theories of socialization. Transcending dualism and the hierarchies of oppositional and evolutionary thinking do not rest on nostalgic images of the past, nor on essentializing specific character traits or values belonging to particular groups of people, such as women or indigenous peoples. It is related to material cultures, it is related to family patterns of early socialization, and it is related to choices of lifestyles.

As Native American communities have always maintained a critical distance from the psychological, intellectual, social, or economic ideals of bourgeois Western society, in its programmatic proposals the National Museum of the American Indian is at the intellectual forefront of shifting scientific and epistemological paradigms. Having the courage to stay in this territory of intellectual uncertainty will be the greatest challenge to the National Museum of the American Indian. For all of us, I hope it will succeed.

NOTES

1. Quoted material in this section is from literature published by the NMAI.

2. Jos van Ussel, *Sexualunterdrückung* (1977), and Norbert Elias, *Über den Prozess der Zivilisation* (1939).

3. Bartoleme de Las Casas, *Brief Account of the Devastation of the Indies* (1542).

4. *Requerimiento, The Spanish Conquest in America and Its Relation to the History of Slavery and to the Government of Colonies* (ca. 1512).

5. On this exclusion philosophers such as Fichte, Kant, and Hegel agree, although from somewhat different perspectives.

6. "Indians should sever their tribal relations and take up abode outside the reservation and then pursue the customs and habits of civilization," quoted in *Encyclopedia of North American Indians.*

7. Locke and Hume seem in agreement in designating non-Western, nonwhite people to primitive and inferior positions.

8. Quoted in George Horse Capture, "An American Indian Perspective," in *Seeds of Change: A Quincentennial Commemoration,* Herman Viola and Carolyn Margolis, eds. (Washington, D.C., and London: Smithsonian Institution Press, 1991).

9. Locke, quoted in Celia Brickman, *Aboriginal Populations in the Mind: Race and Primitivity in Psychoanalysis* (New York: Columbia University Press, 2003).

10. Quoted in Brickman, *Aboriginal Populations.*

11. Secretary of the Interior in 1871, quoted in Carolyn Merchant, *Reinventing Eden: The Fate of Nature in Western Culture* (New York and London: Routledge, 2003).

12. Jürgensen Thomsen is quoted in this section. See Jörgen Jensen, *Thomsen's Museum* (1992).

13. This quote gives the title to Celia Brickman's recent book. In the same vein of the content of the unconscious, feminist theory has claimed that femininity represents the unconscious of men and of society.

14. In the nineteenth and twentieth centuries, generations of Aboriginal children in Australia, of Native American children in the United States, and Roma children in Europe were taken from their families to be assimilated into white Western society.

15. Jette Sandahl, *Proper Objects Among Other Things* (1995) or *Fluid Boundaries and False Dichotomies* (2003).

16. The work of Evelyn Fox Keller heavily influenced the epistemological positions of the Women's Museum.

17. For our part, we hope the NMAI will not just be the National Museum of the American Indian, but the *International* Museum of the American Indian, a resource for European museums holding Native American collections.

18. In our case, possible alliances, pacts, and mutual reconciliations are lent a hand and given authority by the most beautiful new building in the country, with the most imaginative technological equipment and the snazziest design.

The Waterfall Court at the Canadian Museum of Civilization. Gatineau, Quebec.
Photo by Harry Foster, 1993. © Canadian Museum of Civilization.

GEORGE F. MacDONALD

Director Emeritus, Canadian Museum of Civilization, Gatineau, Quebec

Native Voice
at the Canadian Museum of Civilization

I AM VERY PLEASED TO HAVE BEEN ASKED TO PRESENT MY THOUGHTS on the role of museums, national museums in particular, in the portrayal of indigenous cultures. Opening a new national museum here in the nation's capital will truly establish a new milestone of aboriginal world heritage. Such museums are designed and built to last for centuries, which puts them in a class of their own as civic facilities.

I will begin my comments with a reflection on my own experience with a new national history museum in the capital of Canada a decade and a half ago. Its subsequent performance provides some indication of what might be expected for the future of the magnificent museum in which we find ourselves today. Indeed, the National Museum of the American Indian and the Canadian Museum of Civilization share many similarities, from their spectacular and evocative architecture by Douglas Cardinal (Blackfoot) to their emphasis on First Nations telling their own histories.

Beginning in the 1960s, many museums throughout North America began collecting contemporary Native art to add to their predominantly nineteenth-century collections. This curatorial shift coincided with the end of the decline of Native art that had characterized the first six decades of the twentieth century. A new dynamic came into play that has transformed many North American museums from their previous role as repositories of past cultures to dynamos of new creativity based on traditional models and inspirations.

The earliest example of the commercialization of aboriginal art in Canada actually started in the late 1950s with the production and marketing of Inuit sculptures through a Government of Canada program. Under the guidance of James A. Houston, the government-appointed Baffin Island administrator and a trained artist himself, stone-block printmaking was introduced to the Cape Dorset Co-operative. From there it spread throughout the Inuit communities of the Northwest Territories. Communities of hunters in the Canadian Arctic were being relocated to permanent settlements that offered little paid employment. The result was the creation of literally hundreds of thousands of images on paper as well as in stone, bone, and ivory that documented the passing of the last major hunting lifestyle in North America. Thousands of those artworks were added to the ethnological collections of the Canadian Museum of Civilization. Many of the sculptures have been subsequently transferred to the Prince of Wales Museum in Yellowknife, and they eventually will be returned to a museum being planned for the new territory of Nunavut.

The Inuit phenomenon was financially successful, and a similar attempt to form art co-operatives among Indian artists across Canada led to the launch of the Central Indian Marketing Services, headquartered in Ottawa. Indian artists came from more diverse backgrounds and did not share a common language as did the Inuit, and they chose instead to work directly with commercial galleries in urban centers. Norval Morrisseau (Ojibwe) drew from mythological and shamanic images to create the Legend Painting School, or Woodland Art Style, which has since been adopted by hundreds of younger artists. By the late 1960s, museum collections of Indian art began to burgeon, both through donations of private collections and by direct purchases of works from the scores of commercial galleries that sprang up across Canada.

The robust development of contemporary Indian and Inuit art in Canada began in the late 1950s and climaxed in 1967 at the Montreal Expo, which marked the centennial of the Confederation of Canada. Expo '67 initiated a cultural revolution that marked the transition from the colonial to the post-colonial era in Canada. The opening of the Canadian Museum of Civilization, the National Gallery of Canada, and a score of other sizable museum projects across the country within the next quarter century was part of that revolution. The post-colonial museums were markedly different in both their architecture and their contents. A corresponding shift also occurred in museum collection and display practices.

The post-colonial, or more generally, post-modern perspective, is more complex, more multifaceted, and more inclusive than the previous single-perspective model based on Western values of rationalism and colonialism. This newer perspective promotes more intercultural understanding, more intimacy and sharing of histories, and more mutual trust and respect than was possible in earlier museum presentations, which polarized indigenous and colonial perspectives. The opening of the National Museum of the American Indian on the National Mall in Washington clearly represents a further step in the shift toward the integration of New World history into the history of mankind. The location and potent statement of the building itself provides that guarantee.

In my own example from Canada, the Canadian Museum of Civilization (CMC) and Pierre Elliot Trudeau, then prime minister of Canada, convinced Parliament to fund construction of a new home for its historical collections in Ottawa. As a result, I was recalled from sabbatical leave at the Museum of Anthropology at the University of British Columbia in Vancouver to become the new building project director. A series of developments in the museums of British Columbia over the previous two decades provided me with a new perspective on the presentation of Native peoples' histories to an international audience.

Mungo Martin, a Kwakwaka'wakw master carver of totem poles, had been employed by the Provincial Museum of British Columbia since the late 1950s to demonstrate his skills to those visiting Thunderbird Park and the museum, which was then housed in the Parliament Buildings in Victoria. Wilson Duff, the museum's ethnologist, arranged for many other Native carvers to copy examples of poles in the museum's collection that were no longer safe to stand in the park. The visitors enjoyed the demonstration of a living art tradition, and the carving shed became a major focus of the museum's interpretive program.

At almost the same time, the University of British Columbia hired the Haida artist Bill Reid as well as Henry Hunt, a Kwakwaka'wakw apprentice to Mungo Martin, to undertake the reconstruction of Haida dwellings, a mortuary house, and poles based on ones that Reid, Duff, Harry Hawthorne, and others had collected from the Haida village of Ninstints a few years before. In 1972, a new museum was opened on the campus of the University of British Columbia, and the village structures and poles were relocated to the museum site. The museum complex was an instant success with visitors, which prompted me to spend a sabbatical year there in 1980 and 1981 to study how this emphasis on living traditions could be applied to a larger-scaled museum that dealt with more than five hundred Native nations and was designed for ten times the number of visitors.

Another influential museum model that had been planned for millions of visitors a year was the National Museum of Anthropology and History in Mexico City, which opened in 1965. It celebrated the achievements of the pre-Columbian cultures of that country on a scale and architectural style that was truly memorable. The message of the continuity from the past to the living cultures of Mexico was less successful, in my view, than were the glories of the pre-Columbian past. The ethnography galleries were physically separated on an upper floor of the building from the archaeological ones, and many visitors gave them only a cursory glance, or avoided them entirely. Nevertheless, the overall effect of the visit was a shift in attitude to the view that the cultures of the Olmec, the Maya, and the Aztec, among others, were equal to those of ancient Egypt, China, or Greece. An attitudinal change in the perception of international visitors was achieved that affected the presentation of aboriginal histories throughout the Americas.

When we began to plan the Ottawa facility, we circulated a questionnaire across the country that, among other things, probed the attitudes of Canadians towards our Native peoples. The results were depressing. We received mostly negative responses that were rooted in old prejudices and Hollywood stereotypes. It was clear that few Canadians had ever met or even seen Indian or Inuit people from different parts of the country. The survey helped us reposition both exhibition and cultural presentation styles to address these stereotypes. Judging from the results a decade and a half after the Canadian Museum of Civilization opened its doors, it is clear that this museum has had a strong positive impact on more than ten million visitors who have toured the exhibits and witnessed the presentations of Native culture. The museum's approach has also helped sustain the level of visitors above 1.2 million per year and the decline from opening year figures that most museums experience.

The first permanent exhibition to open in 1989 was the West Coast-style village within the enormous space of the CMC's Grand Hall. It is perhaps the largest example of the visible storage approach pioneered by the Museum of Anthropology in which the total collection is on public display. The objective here was to incorporate into its largest public space more than thirty totem poles that the CMC held within its collections. It was at the same time a conscious acknowledgment that the cultures of the West Coast were masters of dramatic performance and that the totem poles, painted house fronts, and enormous war canoes, as well as having specific functions, were also essential props in the production of their own theatrical traditions. To accommodate this level of performance, it became clear that we would need to meet challenging requirements for dressing rooms, washroom facilities, and a greenroom space that were conveniently located for the thousands of individuals from diverse cultural backgrounds who would animate the Grand Hall with their presentations.

With the realization that we were venturing into new territory for museums, with live performances by appropriate representatives of different cultural styles that required careful planning of adjacencies and amenities, we sent members of our design team to Disney World and Epcot Center in Florida to study their highly successful performance spaces as well as their customer services standards and staff training programs. This action brought the wrath of the museum community down on our heads, as Disney is often considered the antithesis of traditional museums. What motivated us was our sense that something along the lines of Disney's visitor services delivery methods were needed to support our central message of intercultural understanding rather than one of pure entertainment.

The crisis point occurred in the fabrication of the six plank houses of the West Coast tribes that occupied the immense Grand Hall of the new building. As the time frame for the opening grew short, the construction managers strongly expressed their doubts that the various teams of Native carvers and carpenters could deliver the house structures on site in time for the opening date. They presented alternative plans to make the houses of standard building materials on designs done by their own draftsmen and framed by local workmen with decorative effects later added by exhibit installation teams. I resisted the pressure to abandon the Native production teams spread over a thousand miles of coastline, some three thousand miles from Ottawa. I was secure in my own prior experience with the craftsmanship they offered. When the time came to bless and purify the tribal houses just before the museum opened, it was evident that the degree of authenticity they had achieved was unique and would inspire performances that would take place within them for many decades to come.

A side benefit of this approach was seen in the degree to which the whole community for each tribal house became engaged with the artists in re-creating a complex activity that had not been practiced for more than a century. That exercise brought elders and young people together in an activity that empowered both groups and led to many subsequent house-building projects and major art commissions for their own community use. Elders revived old ceremonies for the dedication of the structures, which encouraged the youth to take more interest in both their ancestral languages and traditions.

Another major issue was whose "voice" would carry the message of the exhibition—that of the curator or that of the Native person whose story was being told. This became of major importance in the First Peoples Hall, which was under the guidance of a committee made up of roughly equal numbers of staff curators and First Nations cultural representatives. It was clear from the outset that the basic nature of the two voices were in sharp contrast. The curatorial voice was that of the art historian and social scientist, which tends toward general statements of culture, relatively devoid of named individuals and their stories. Native voice is much more direct and engaging, and it gained ground with the committee until the concept of a "dual voice" took center stage. The public was very responsive to this approach and commented positively on it in surveys.

Visitors wanted to have the hard facts of time and place that were provided by the archaeologist, but they also appreciated the intricate and rich story lines of the tribal historian, singer, or artist. As might be expected, mythology added a great deal to the understanding of Native artworks. Donors and patrons were especially attracted to the mythological context of a particular artist's work. Several art commissions and donations resulted from conversations that took place between a visitor and an aboriginal artist who was working with the museum. A case in point was the work of the Haida master artist Bill Reid.

Over the space of a few years, patrons from across the country presented to the CMC commissioned works by Reid and others, worth many millions of dollars. The first one was the original plaster for the eighteen-foot-high killer whale sculpture that Reid titled *King of the Undersea World*. A gift from a Vancouver family, it dramatically anchored the entry end of the Grand Hall. That was quickly followed by the plaster pattern of *The Spirit of Haida Gwaii*, which was commissioned by the Government of Canada for its new embassy in Washington on the other side of the Mall from the National Museum of the American Indian. That piece was positioned at the Ottawa River end of the Grand Hall. An even larger work by Reid, a bronze twenty-six feet in length, had to be mounted on an outside wall of the CMC since no interior wall could accommodate it.

Public exposure to his work at the CMC led to a demand for more information about the artist. A large program of text and images was offered on the CMC website, and it was further enhanced at his death in 1998. In a subsequent development, the designer of the new $20 bank note for the Bank of Canada in Ottawa saw both the three monumental sculptures by Bill Reid at CMC and his biography on our website, and was motivated to choose his work to represent all of the arts in Canada. More than five billion of these bills will be in circulation during its planned life cycle, which will encourage the establishment of these monumental sculptures as national icons.

The Grand Hall soon became the favorite location in the National Capital Region for the Government of Canada to entertain visiting heads of state and other dignitaries. Most recently, the Grand Hall of the CMC was chosen to stage the state banquet for President George W. Bush on his visit to Canada in late November 2004. It also became the choice of First Nations for the celebration of their successes as well. The Report of the Royal Commission on Aboriginal Peoples was released from its stage in 1996, and the Declaration of the New Territory of Nunavut was made there in 2000. To the museum's delight, Indian and Inuit people throughout the country adopted the Grand Hall as a symbol of their collective histories and pride. Chief Joe Norton of the Mohawk Nation called it "the best Band Council Office in the Nation."

There was little question that museums were creating a new demand for monumental artworks by Iroquois and Inuit artists as well as those from the Northwest Coast. Human stone slab figures, or Inukshuk, began to appear in front of many Canadian museums. Iroquois sculptures that began as soapstone carvings became massive groupings on a grand scale in the works of David General and others.

Large murals by aboriginal artists were another requirement of the new museums, and the CMC was no exception. A large work by Norval Morrisseau came to grace one of the few straight walls in the reading room of the library in Cardinal's building. It was Morrisseau who single-handedly established the Woodland Art style, which inspired more than one hundred other artists from the Eastern Woodlands to depict the legends of the Cree and the Ojibwe in oils and acrylics. The CMC also commissioned Chipewyan artist Alex Janvier and his son Dean to paint a complex mural on an eighty-foot dome at the end of the Grand Hall. The commission, titled *Morning Star*, required a complex scaffold with ladders and drape cloths; many who viewed the work-in-progress compared the experience to what must have been the thrill of seeing the Sistine Chapel while Michelangelo painted it.

The theme Janvier chose for his ceiling mural was the morning star as seen by a youth who had just undergone fasting and initiation as a hunter in traditional times. As Janvier explained, the initiate, driven by hunger and lack of sleep, developed supersensitive hearing, by which he noted every sound in the forest, and visual acuity, by which he could see beyond every-day reality into a cosmic vision that would last a lifetime. His own vision was divided into four parts, representing the four ages of Native history in vivid color. The first was a pre-Contact world, followed by the clash of cultures of the Old and New Worlds. That conflict led to a massive dying off of both Native cultures and their bearers, until finally a new age of re-energized Native cultures and optimism took hold. The near-perfect marriage of the mural with the architecture continues to inspire photographers to attempt to capture the spirit of the place.

Although the consultation process had been used before in successfully developing First Nations' exhibits in many provincial museums across Canada, none attempted to get a consensus from more than a million aboriginal and Métis inhabitants at one time. A major lesson we learned from this large-scale approach was that there are profound cultural differences among the more than one hundred language groups and five hundred distinct aboriginal communities in Canada. The consultations required to develop mutually agreeable perspectives on history took a great deal of time and resources. The meetings took more than a decade to conclude, and resulted in at least three phases of redesign of the First Peoples exhibitions. The last gallery opened to the public in 2003. Based on this experience, I much admire the fact that the exhibitions at the NMAI were complete on opening day.

Throughout the period of negotiating the question of voice and the selection of themes that would be emphasized in the First Peoples Hall, the issue of repatriation was also a matter of intense discussion among delegations from various First Nations and the staff of the CMC. At one point in the late 1990s, more than one hundred and fifty nations were on the negotiation list, with the vast majority from British Columbia, and they became linked to treaty negotiations involving both the federal and provincial governments.

The first completed negotiations were with the Nisga'a of British Columbia, who requested that cultural objects from the CMC and the Royal British Columbia Museum be on the negotiating table along with timber, mineral, and fishing rights as well as land and monetary compensation. It was recognized that repatriation, particularly of human remains and sacred objects, puts enormous stress on the communities that receive the returned objects. Mere preservation of the objects can become burdensome if security and fire prevention measures are absent. Curatorial skills are often lacking within the communities. To address this situation, the CMC instituted a museology training program for First Nations' students in 1993. A decade later almost one hundred Native people have graduated from this program and have the range of museum and collection management skills needed to ensure the preservation of the collections for the foreseeable future

Another experiment that aimed to address the question of access by Native peoples to their own heritage was launched in 1994 when the CMC website went online. A decade later, some fifty million visits have been made to the site. More than fifty virtual exhibits are currently online, and many thousands of Native artifact images and historical photographs have been digitized and are online. Some exhibits were designed to be only virtual ones, while others depict actual exhibits long after they have been taken down. Visit www.Civilization.ca and search for a list of exhibits that have appeared in the museum over the past fifteen years. The NMAI plans to go farther by envisioning a "fourth museum" that will create new levels of outreach to indigenous communities, once the Mall museum is fully operational.

The CMC web staff has worked extensively with the SchoolNet project of the federal government, which has satellite access to almost all Native schools throughout Canada. The Canadian Heritage Information Network has been a partner with the CMC in building archaeological site inventories and ethnological databases since 1972. This eventually led to the Virtual Museum of Canada, which contains Native art and cultural collections from more than a dozen museums across the country. The CMC has recently partnered with the Museum of Anthropology at the University of British Columbia and a number of First Nations' museums in that province, as well as with several other museums in Alaska and Washington State and the NMAI to create an extensive database for Northwest Coast Native studies. Other such collective databases will inevitably follow for other aboriginal groups.

The events surrounding the opening of the National Museum of the American Indian are being made available live on the World Wide Web. This is one more indication that a major new facility is taking a leadership role in the protection and further development of the languages and cultures of the First Nations of the Americas.

BERNICE L. MURPHY

Vice President, International Council of Museums (ICOM-Paris)

ESTABLISHING CONNECTIONS, RELEASING CAPACITIES: A REFLECTION ON THE RESURGENCE OF INDIGENOUS ARTS IN AUSTRALIA

IT IS IMPORTANT FIRST TO HONOR THE INAUGURATION of the National Museum of the American Indian, which provides a new energy center within the Smithsonian Institution and a focal point in Washington for a transformed sense of interconnecting histories. I acknowledge the Piscataway peoples, on whose lands we have gathered, and all Native peoples who treasure their distinctive traditions as well as their forebears, who are commemorated in this arresting new center for cultural heritage.

I also affirm the desire articulated in the NMAI's development documents to project the values of *living traditions* of cultural creativity, as this new museum emphatically conveys to the wider world. It is from this point of connection with *evolving creativity* that I contribute as a guest at the historic inauguration of this new institution in Washington.

I do not speak *for* indigenous people from my own country, Australia. That role belongs to the many different peoples concerned. My approach here is from the perspective of a curator and former art museum director who has been involved museologically in integrating indigenous creativity into the panorama of contemporary artistic creativity evident in different contexts across the world today.

John Mawurndjul, *Man Djabu at Mumeka*, 2003–04. Museum of Contemporary Art, Sydney, Australia, and Maningrida Arts and Culture. Purchased 2003. © The artist. Photo by Eric Sierins.

For many years in Australia, I have been interested in opportunities for bringing indigenous representations and indigenous curatorship into our public galleries and museums. This could not be accomplished through the practices of existing institutions alone. New connections had to be made, stretching beyond museums and involving near and far-distant communities. Relationships needed to be established, so that interpretive projects and collections could be shaped in new ways, bringing indigenous perspectives into our mainstream institutions.

The result of many events forming a confluence over more than two decades is that we now have fine indigenous curators in our leading state and national museums, art museums, and the National Gallery of Australia. I believe that they will become important contact persons and colleagues in the future, and hope that you will learn directly from them about their work and evolving ideas.

Interest in Aboriginal art in Australian art museums can be traced back at least to the 1950s. However, the efflorescence of Aboriginal art in our museum exhibitions, collecting, and public programming, and its presence in art activity internationally, has occurred only since the early 1980s.

This paper has four themes. First, I sketch an outline of some significant exhibitions in which Australian indigenous art began to appear strongly in museums and galleries in the early 1980s. I indicate the powerful position such projects have gained in the spectrum of contemporary art today, steadily influencing collections—although the latter is a subject that would require a fuller account than is possible here. Second, I seek to highlight some of the evolving processes and contexts underlying such change. Third, I offer a personal reflection on changing paradigms and positioning of indigenous creativity over a quarter-century of recent development. Fourth—and I assume most important for audiences in North America—I will address some key challenges facing indigenous art and artists.

Proprietary Knowledge

What can properly be known or interpreted by anyone outside the members of a particular people or culture? I raise this issue early to pay respect to the idea that indigenous or First Nations people worldwide inherit unique identity-conferring and historical connections to specific lands, sites, waterways, and resources—connections maintained even through physical separation from such sites. Moreover, the ritual or customary life associated with particular places, phenomena, creatures, and persons involves restricted knowledge, as well as knowledge that may be shared with others.

Coming from a background in art rather than anthropology, I have been comfortable working in situations of restricted or incomplete knowledge for several reasons. First, art images are readily understood as partial but also special kinds of subjectively encoded phenomena. They are not presumed to "represent" persons, communities, or lifeways in a merely referential or ethnographically normative sense. This does not mean, however, any lack of interest in deepening layers of knowledge (social, communal, scientific, even psychological knowledge) as a supplement to experience.

Inside/Outside Dimensions of Cultural Forms

It has been useful in my work as a curator to consider that cultural forms emerging from specific communities, especially indigenous communities, have strongly felt "inside" dimensions in contrast to more external, or "outside," dimensions. From the perspective of art, it is the "outside" dimensions that are attended to most often. Yet an art vantage point recognizes that there are always further, graduated "inside" dimensions to visual forms and that these have intimate connections to other forms, such as dance, music, or song. We can never fully know, however, the "inside" dimensions from a producer's point of view; we may only have partial knowledge about these things.

My suggestions about an art perspective would be the following: that an acceptance of partial or incomplete knowledge, a greater emphasis on the space of public exchange, and an anticipation of unfixable, multiple, and even ephemeral experiences are crucial distinctions between the mentality of art and that of anthropology. These two disciplinary worlds have traditionally very different expectations of and vantage points on both experience and knowledge.

Positive Philosophical Uncertainty

Extending the idea of acceptance of partial knowledge, my attention was caught by a page in the NMAI master facilities planning report of 1991—an exhaustive and detailed document entitled *The Way of the People*. I was particularly interested in the one-page framework developed by Dr. Rina Swentzell (Santa Clara Pueblo) concerning Native American philosophical assumptions.[1]

Dr. Swentzell highlights an epistemology of "relative truth"—in contrast, for example, to a philosophical absolutism that would elevate truth above human community as an abstract and unvarying concept. She indicates further the importance of "subjective knowing" and situated truth—a sense of truth that depends on context and is responsive to a "multiuniverse" in which "many worlds [are] possible."

The emphases on multiple possibilities within the same situation, and on knowledge as intersubjective and socially situated (rather than abstract and universal) struck me as close to some of the orientations that a contemporary art mentality brings to the encounter with indigenous cultures. I think again of mental attitudes that are rather different from the traditions historically brought by the social sciences—even the importantly self-reforming discourses of anthropology today. I do not wish, however, to diminish the subtlety of how anthropology is evolving or to engage in simplistic turf wars. That is not helpful or productive from my point of view.

Living Cultures, Creative Opportunities

I would like to present a few examples of the striking changes that have occurred within the art world in terms of the inclusion of indigenous arts as "living cultures." Let us begin with art from the tropical north of Australia—Kuninjku art of Western Arnhem Land.

The 13th Biennale of Sydney, staged across Sydney's two main art museums in the year 2000, contained a large room that was powerful in its provocative response to the idea of a shrinking world system of contemporary art. While Yoko Ono had taken over the main entrance court of the state gallery (with an installation of one hundred slender orange trees emerging from wooden coffins),[2] across town at the Museum of Contemporary Art on the edge of Sydney Harbor (my former museum), a constellation of paintings and objects in a seventeen-meter gallery space established an un-forgettable presence in the Biennale. The room contained a series of large bark paintings by John Mawurndjul accompanied by a series of wooden sculptures of *mimi* (spirit) figures from sixteen of his contemporary Yolngu (or Aboriginal) artists of the far north of Australia.

These works were made by individuals living in a multilingual[3] commu-nity of peoples connected to lands around the township of Maningrida, near the coastline facing Papua New Guinea (north) and Indonesia (north-west). Thus, alongside a selection of works by well-known "professional artists" from around the world, drawing on visual traditions of a mere few centuries—even decades—the 2000 Biennale of Sydney also presented work by artists who live within continuous cultural traditions stretching back many thousands of years,[4] from communities that still maintain rich cus-toms across Arnhem Land, east of Darwin.[5]

Changing Paradigms: Challenges of Interpretation

A central issue for this paper is: How did such a remarkable transformation come about in a matter of a few decades? How did work by Australian in-digenous artists (that is, artists of Aboriginal and Torres Strait Islander backgrounds) move out of any enclosure within ethnographical frame-works—held largely in our natural history museums—and became incorpo-rated into the domain of contemporary art? What underlies the fundamen-tal changes that have brought to life in our art galleries and museums so many works of astonishingly transformed scale, means, power, and presence?

An important emphasis is needed here about these bark paintings and *mimi* sculptures from Kuninjku clans in Arnhem Land—an insistence that runs counter to two possible tendencies in audience response that would undermine a full understanding of the terms of engagement. I speak first against the mythologizing impulse that would shift these works into a space of separation, maintaining an inviolable cleavage from works around them by asserting their connection to customary religious law. Second, I speak against any anxiety about the works' possible cultural corruption in their encounter with the terms of international "art." There is no reason to an-ticipate that the works are diminished in cultural "authenticity" by the translations—in scale, formal elaboration, textures, and details—involved in moving towards a broad public audience. In fact, it is patronizing for outsiders to assume that these works are not shaped by their authors in self-conscious ways, with an intentional control of distinct iconography and internal meanings, while they are also directed to the external audiences whose attention they seek to arouse.

The key points I wish to stress here are as follows. The new exhibition spaces and creative opportunities opened up for these artists over two decades in Australia have been dramatically productive. Despite the amplitude of distinct and unique traditions from which they are drawn—from creative individuals still leading a traditional life in so-called remote communities—these works are addressed knowingly to an international art audience. They are contextually specific and rhetorically articulate in the present tense. The character of the works, many of which have been commissioned, has been shaped by an anticipated destination and engagement with a (value-creating) external audience. Such enlarged opportunities involve an expansion of the political and cultural desire that stands behind the works. And let there be no mistake about either this implacable political desire or the authentic social agency of these works, no matter how much they may enter the tangle of values that surround an art system and its networks of commodification.

The steps by which the transformation of exhibition opportunities for indigenous artists was achieved in Australia comprise a story of some twenty-five years (certainly as far as my own working life and some involvement in these processes have been concerned). The various developments that occurred, however, rest upon a quite simply stated approach, one that has provided a framework for my work as a curator of contemporary art since the late 1970s. It runs as follows, in two parts—the first is a premise; the second is a principle for action.

The premise: Indigenous art, no matter how specific its originating cultural background, may also be regarded fully as contemporary art—that is to say, made in the world, of the world, and in dialogue with the world. Accordingly, the principal guiding action must be: Treat indigenous artists as artists. This means establishing the spaces and opportunities for their cre-

ativity to act in the present tense in the public sphere, with the same open-
ness, contextual sensitivity, and imaginative diversity that any living artists
deserve. Their own obligations to communal and kinship imperatives, and
to alternative knowledge and belief systems, are issues that can be attended
to along the way. It is presumptuous for outsiders to make judgments about
these in advance.

The "Papunya Movement" of the Western Desert

We now move away from the tropical north to discuss a similarly dramatic
example of work that emerged in the 1970s from another area of creativity hundreds of miles southwest of Darwin—paintings from the vast dry
center of the Australian continent and the great Western Desert lands stretching north and west of Alice Springs. I refer here to the so-called "Papunya
Movement."[6]

Work associated with the settlement of Papunya—a new form of painting in acrylics on board and later on canvas—was featured prominently in
the famous *Dreamings* exhibition at the Asia Society Galleries in New York,
in 1988 (Australia's bicentennial year, incidentally). The *Dreamings* exhibition seemingly broke all records for attendance at the Asia Society Galleries.[7]

Here I want to reach back earlier and touch briefly on my personal history of presenting Aboriginal art in art museums. While this began in 1978
(with an exhibition of Australian art in Indonesia),[8] I want to discuss a more
significant occasion that occurred three years later.

In 1981, I inaugurated a series of biennial projects in Australian contemporary art, designed to occur in alternate years with the Biennale of Sydney (begun in 1973).[9] The new series of biennial exhibitions was inaugurated under the title *Australian Perspecta*, and I organized and curated the first
two (in 1981 and 1983), exploring the work of some one hundred and fifty
artists.

What most caught the public's attention was the startling presence and
role of Aboriginal art in both projects. In 1981, the scale and power of
three large paintings on canvas from Papunya, installed on a long wall in the
Sydney art museum's prime space, which had previously been identified with

large visiting exhibitions from abroad, took many people by surprise. Here
was Aboriginal art from so-called traditional[10] Aboriginal communities not
only in the company of a rather large panorama of recent art drawn from
the whole country, but also "speaking"[11] in the same space. What was so
surprising in 1981—but now is so familiar as to be expected—was that
"traditional" Aboriginal art (or art based in continuing cultural practice
while also evolving new forms) was presented as part of contemporary art.
It was framed not as ethnographic productivity (yielding artifacts), but as
contemporary creativity (yielding art).

The second *Australian Perspecta* exhibition in 1983 turned back to the
"older" (but also adaptive) form of bark paintings from Arnhem Land. An
opportunity I was able to create in the second *Perspecta* exhibition opened a
door that introduced Djon Mundine (Bundjalung people, New South Wales)[12]
as an indigenous curator in an art museum context. An invitation to Djon
to shape the Aboriginal representation from Arnhem Land in 1983 yielded
discussion with elders in the Ramingining community, where he was then
based as an art adviser. Through his consultation with Jinang elder David
Malangi (1927–1999), a remarkable cycle of works from this senior painter
and ritual leader was commissioned. The invitation enabled Malangi to present not one or two discrete items but a linked suite of works. This contribution to a prominent art event in Sydney from within an alternative cultural framework represented an affirmative step in the evolution of
contemporary art in Australia.

What I would stress about my own role at this point is that I never se-
lected works on the basis of aesthetics alone, nor did I act autonomously. I
first sought the guidance of people working most closely with Aboriginal
communities and artists (the Aboriginal Arts Board in the first instance;
later, the successive art advisers who had been or were still based at Papunya).

Meanwhile, I was developing what proved to be a prolonged collegial dialogue with Djon Mundine, who was working in the far north from 1979[13]
onwards. He was based first on the island of Milingimbi, then briefly at
Maningrida,[14] and then for thirteen years at Ramingining. The only art adviser with an indigenous background, who at that time moved into the wider

world of institutional negotiations across the country, Djon Mundine was developing as a kind of curator-in-the-field. His direct work with indigenous artists, whose interests served as his primary orientation, enabled me to shift the terms of curatorship in transformative ways as far as museums were concerned. The second *Australian Perspecta* exhibition in 1983 facilitated the introduction of indigenous curatorship directly into a large exhibition, before any on-staff professional positions had been created for indigenous curators in art museums.

Turning back to the case of Papunya for a moment, I again wish to raise the crucial issue of authenticity. There was a period when some cultural critics in the 1980s[15] strongly argued that the circulation of Papunya paintings for exhibition and sale constituted a perilous threat to authenticity and a dilution of Aboriginal cultural integrity. On the contrary (as Professor Fred Myers has argued in the case of the Pintupi[16] men from lands furthest west), paintings always carry a political desire for autonomy and independence through the signs, embedded meaning, and ritual authority—the "law"— that the paintings directly convey to a wider audience:

> Part of the capacity of these intercultural objects to represent, or to say something, lies in their engagement not only with the Aboriginal system of meaning and social relations but also with available discourses and institutions of the arts in the dominant Euro-Australian society.[17]

When the Asia Society's *Dreamings* exhibition gained prominent attention in New York in 1988, it was but one event among many in a complex and cumulative process. The much-lauded success of this venture was the outcome of a series of transformational shifts in opportunity and communication that had occurred first inside Australia, whereby paintings originally from traditional life and ritual contexts began to move out in new forms and materials to reach a mainstream audience (seen as the key to political power over indigenous futures). The paintings' characteristics changed because of the conscious efforts of Aboriginal artists to address a distant audience.

Nevertheless, as Fred Myers indicates, this engagement was motivated by a desire to protect and renew cultural traditions and regain proprietary rights and access to clan lands, upon which all aspects of cultural organization, law, and mutually connecting social identity and kinship are based.

Exhibitions as Instruments
of Cultural Communication and Evolving Creativity

There is a conventional taxonomic profile by which not only the activities but also the mentality of museums can be described. The repetition of this profile produces a restrictive identity for the institutional character of "the museum," both historically and operationally. The "museum template," if you will, drawn repeatedly by commentators and critical theorists, gives a primary place to collections, a secondary position to displays and educational activities, and a tertiary position to exhibitions.

The tenacity of this historical template restricts even the best-intentioned efforts to create a different map of development. What is missing from the "acquisition, preservation, interpretation" model is the complex role and agency of exhibitions in museums' potential as social institutions and cultural interpreters. It could even be argued that exhibitions have come to distinguish museums in their public interface more than collections themselves.

A more general museological point I would make is much broader: Museum collections are not auto-productive constellations of meaning. They do not self-illuminate, either internally or to a wider public. It is through exhibitions, above all, that museums most effectively disclose themselves to a public as meaning-making institutions. Moreover, I have long regarded exhibitions as the ideal research and development arm of a reflexive approach to the collection function.[18]

Exhibitions offer the following dynamic opportunities for a museum's thinking and development:

• Presentation of new subjects and fields of interest (thought and phenomena as well as objects)
• Dialogic engagement with diverse communities and constituencies

• Exploration of progressive, new interpretative possibilities
• Recontextualization of objects that have been segregated from their originating contexts
• Production of new constellations of objects and experiences that may themselves open new possibilities for reinterpreting and reengaging long-known material, developing new ideas for future projects
• Stimulation of new audiences and sources of patronage for collection development.

Thinking particularly of the opportunities and values that the National Museum of the American Indian seeks to nurture, exhibitions would provide an important vehicle for enlisting the direct involvement of Native artists and communities in engaged self-representation. This would help the NMAI fulfill one of its primary missions: the "preservation" and "perpetuation" of "living cultures."

The important points of emphasis I would make in summary are on evolving events of inclusion and representation, in which indigenous presence, agency, and self-determining representation—as well as diversified professional experience and opportunity for artists and curators—have been steadily advanced.

It is worth noting by way of comparison that we have as yet no national museum of Aboriginal and Torres Strait Islander culture, although we do have an exhibiting center, the Tandanya, the National Aboriginal Cultural Institute based in Adelaide. There may yet be a strong desire to create a national institution for indigenous culture in Australia, comparable to the National Museum of the American Indian in the United States. One of the most interesting reasons for the current delay of such an outcome, in my view, is that Australian indigenous artists have successfully pursued an engaged self-representation in existing museums, challenging the dominant cultural and social mainstream, and they have been increasingly valued for their production within mainstream institutions.

It was impossible to predict twenty years ago that Aboriginal artists would seize opportunities and enter the creative spaces opened to them—and here

I must make a final, important mention of the role of urban artists. No one could have imagined in the 1970s that Aboriginal culture would impact so strongly on Australia's evolving self-interpretation of its history, or that urban indigenous art's critical agency would expand and change the scope of indigenous art's reference points (for example, in reinterpreting historical archives) in such far-reaching ways.

Exhibitions under the aegis and ethos of contemporary art have been the critical arena within which Aboriginal and Torres Strait Islander artists (and just as importantly, indigenous curators) have gained presence and agency. Meanwhile, the relationship among the collecting, exhibiting, and interpreting functions of museums has become ever more dynamic and complex, enabling museums to be both a primary site and a medium through which evolving interpretations and critical revisions have occurred in Australia's self-understanding as a nation.

I return finally to my simply stated guideline for the safeguarding and continuity of living cultures: Treat indigenous artists from urban or remote communities as fully self-conscious artists. Build the same experiences and opportunities for them—with the same support structures and complete professionalism—as for any other artists from all parts of the world. Doing so means being sensitive to their interests and needs—and that is where cultural specificity comes into play—rather than beginning with any ethnographical precepts or generalized expectations.

From the vantage point of an art museum: Treat artists as artists! Everything else may be developed on the basis of this fundamental orientation.

NOTES

1. "Native American Philosophical Assumptions," guidelines developed by Dr. Rina Swentzell (Santa Clara Pueblo) for discussion by participants in the Santa Fe consultation, is included in the unpublished document entitled, *The Way of the People: National Museum of the American Indian* (Washington, D.C.: Smithsonian Institution, Office of Design and Construction, 1991), 96–97. See Master Facilities Programming, Phase I, Revised Draft Report/ODC Project No. 902003, November 22, 1991.

2. Yoko Ono's *Ex It*, an installation conceived originally for a medieval building in Valen-

cia, Spain, in 1997, appeared in the *Biennale of Sydney 2000*, Art Gallery of New South Wales, Sydney.

3. Maningrida incorporates a community of a few thousand individuals in the township and surrounding area. Some nine or ten Yolngu (or indigenous) languages are spoken there, making it one of the most linguistically dense areas in the world. Scholarship about Aboriginal and Torres Strait Islander culture is in a considerable state of flux, with data constantly evolving. This is a cautionary reminder about the rather fluid state of statistics when factual information is sought. For some years it has been generally held that there were approximately two hundred Aboriginal languages, with "hundreds" of dialects spoken prior to the rupture of European colonization. See Peter Sutton, "Wik: Aboriginal Society, Territory and Language at Cape Keerweer, Cape York Peninsula," (unpublished doctoral dissertation, University of Queensland, 1978), cited in Peter Sutton, ed. *Dreamings*, (New York: Viking/Asia Society, 1988), 6–7, 260. The work of linguists and more precise research with indigenous speech communities and elders has stimulated progressive revision of the statistical estimates of archaeologists and anthropologists, requiring continual updating of statistics as research proceeds. Anthropologist Luke Taylor's statistics for pre-Contact languages indicate "over 250 different Indigenous languages, comprising about 700 dialect groups." See Luke Taylor, "Introduction," *Painting the Land Story* (Canberra: National Museum of Australia, 1999). Such differences in museum publications from respected Australian anthropologists give an indication of how research is dynamic and constantly evolving.

4. Some stone artifacts found in the region to the far north of Australia have been archaeologically dated to approximately fifty thousand years ago, positing human occupation at least since that time. Scientifically tested sites proving complex human cultural expression (petroglyphs) at rock sites in desert areas further south are more recent, dating to approximately thirty thousand years ago. Meanwhile, the oldest human remains, preserved in dry sands in the southeastern area of the continent, have yielded proof of ritualized human burials thirty to forty thousand years ago. Most notable are the carefully arranged skeletons incorporating ochred bones, found at Lake Mungo, New South Wales, that are dated to thirty thousand years ago. See Sutton, *Dreamings*, 5.

5. "The *Mimi* figure is an ancient theme in the Aboriginal art of western Arnhem Land. As it has been established that certain rock paintings of *mimi* are several thousand years old, the representation of these spirit figures may be the most enduring art tradition known." See Jennifer Hoff and Luke Taylor, "The Mimi Spirit as Sculpture," *Art and Australia* 23, no. 1 (Spring 1985), 73; excerpt reprinted in Ewen McDonald, ed. *Biennale of Sydney 2000* (Sydney: Biennale of Sydney, 2000), 78.

6. The story of the development of Papunya painting, or Western Desert acrylic painting, and its later remarkable progress to world prominence and international appearances in the late 1980s—notably in the *Dreamings* exhibition at the Asia Society Galleries, New York, in 1988 (later shown in Los Angeles and Chicago)—has been thoroughly researched by Fred R. Myers, professor and chair of anthropology at New York University. His research is available in his recent publication, *Painting Culture: The Making of an Aboriginal High*

Art (Durham: Duke University Press, 2002). Professor Myers' important anthropological work in Australia began with fieldwork while he lived with Pintupi people in the central desert country in 1973 and 1974. In his most recent book he reflects upon his three decades of academic work and his continuing contact with Pintupi people. This exhaustive study addresses contemporary Aboriginal culture in Australia and analyzes the movement of paintings from Papunya out into the world. Myers encapsulates the phenomenon as "the making of an Aboriginal high art." Myers introduces but does not adequately explore some issues from the perspective of art (rather than anthropology). He does not go far enough in the direction he has set himself, engaging different terms required through an understanding of curatorial practices, exhibitions such as biennales, and the institutional settings of art and the many spaces where it is publicly experienced. This does not invalidate the important work he has undertaken, but it does leave it incomplete. There is more to be done to supplement Myers' detailed accounting, admitting more perspectives than anthropology has granted in the past.

7. According to Myers, *Dreamings* drew the largest attendance (27,000 visitors) of any exhibit ever held at the Asia Society. See Myers, *Painting Culture*, 237.

8. Pemandangan alam dan Khayal/ *Landscape and Image: A Selection of Australian Art of the 1970s* (Sydney: Australian Gallery Directors Council, 1978), with four venues in Indonesia. This event was rather modest and occurred outside Australia, beyond the periphery of attention at home.

9. My own appointment to the position of curator of contemporary art at the state Art Gallery of New South Wales (AGNSW), Sydney, a position I held from 1979 to 1984, reflected a threshold of changing consciousness in Australian art museums. This was the first curatorial post created by a state or national art gallery that recognized "contemporary art" as a dedicated category of museum activity, with responsibilities that differed from those serving the category of "modern art." The fact that the Biennale of Sydney had been hosted by this same institution since its second edition (in 1976) gave an obvious impetus for the AGNSW to be the first state institution to make such a move.

10. It must be noted that "traditional" is a problematic, unstable term. Tradition forms within all human communities; moreover, its development is an historical process of culture-formation, subject always to dynamics of slow or rapid change. In referring to Australian indigenous communities, "traditional" is often no more than a quick, awkward shorthand to honor the survivalist strength of Aboriginal communities in places "remote" from the major cities in the south and southeast, namely, communities in the center and far north of Australia that are still close to their ancestral lands. No matter what circumstances of colonization have intervened, many of these communities have maintained ceremonial and customary life to a remarkable degree, evolving these traditions to cope with new circumstances. Meanwhile, urban traditions of indigenous culture are constantly evolving and reforming, with a rich play of styles drawing on indigenous, subcultural, mainstream, and global cultural forms.

11. "Speaking" is a volatile term, and I use it with full consciousness of its ambiguity. It also raises profoundly important issues of the fragmentation of cultural representation,

through its segmentation of objects and interpretation by different academic discourses across different kinds of museums, from natural history to ethnography, and further to art museum frameworks. These issues, and the way in which different museographical devices were drawn upon in the *Australian Perspecta* exhibition of 1981 to accompany this new situation, would require a much longer exposition.

12. In the years since 1983, Djon Mundine has become one of the best-known curators in Australia (and one of the most traveled of all Australian museum curators). I would not interpret Djon's work for him. Numerous publications and exhibition projects he has shaped, or to which he has contributed, provide more direct references and access to his ideas and intentions. See, for example, Bernice Murphy and Djon Mundine, eds. *The Native Born: Objects and Representations from Ramingining* (Sydney: Museum of Contemporary Art, 2000).

13. See Susan Jenkins' biographical notes on contributors: "Djon Mundine" in *No Ordinary Place: The Art of David Malangi* (Canberra: National Gallery of Australia, 2004), inside cover.

14. Djon Mundine, "Some People Are Stories," in *No Ordinary Place*, 29.

15. Most uncompromisingly, Tony Fry and Anne-Marie Willis, "Aboriginal Art: Symptom or Success?" *Art in America* (July 1989), 109–17, 159–60.

16. Myers, *Painting Culture*, see esp. chap. 8.

17. Myers, *Painting Culture*, 7.

18. The theoretical positioning of exhibitions as the ideal research and development arm of a museum's collection development, especially for a contemporary institution, was elaborated in Bernice Murphy, *Museum of Contemporary Art: Vision and Context.*

Te Papa at dusk, 1998. Museum of New Zealand Te Papa Tongarewa, Wellington, New Zealand. Photo by Michael Hall.

DAME CHERYLL SOTHERAN

Founding Director, Museum of New Zealand Te Papa Tongarewa

The Museum of New Zealand Te Papa Tongarewa: A Bicultural Model for Museums

Tuatahi

Me whiu atu au he karanga ki nga tangata o te whenua
kua ngaro ratou ki te po
Me koutou nga tangata whenua kei te ora.

Anei te Karanga o te iwi kainga kia koutou

Here is the call to the first people of this land from Maori people of my land

Karanga mai ra nga iwi o te whenua nei
Karanga mai
Karanga mai
Karanga mai

Call me all first Nation tribes [clans] to your land
Call me
Call me

Karanga mai ra koutou te mana whenua o tenei rohe
Karanga mai
Karanga mai
Karanga mai

Call me the people of the tribe [clan] of the land I am now standing on

Haere atu ra nga tini aitua kua wehe atu ki te po
Haere atu ra
Haere atu ra
Haera atu ra

May the sorrows of your ancestors and our ancestors go peacefully into the darkness [or the dark night]

Karangamai ra nga maunga (tei tei tall high) nga awa o koutou

Call me the sacred mountains and the rivers of this land

Karanga mai, tena koe, tenei whare ataahua me te whenua,
Kakahu mai au, tiakina mai au I tenei ra

Oh beautiful house that I stand in and the land it stands on
I call you, I greet you.
Cloak and look after me as a traditional Maori cloak does to the individual

Karanga mai I runga I te Kaupapa o te ra nei

Kia koutou nga kanohi ora
e nga mana e nga reo e nga raurangatira ma
koutou e whakatau ia au
Te nei te mihi kia koutou katoa

IN RECOGNIZING THE HIGH IMPORTANCE TO THE GLOBAL FAMILY of museums that accompanies the opening of the National Museum of the American Indian in Washington, we have an opportunity to see this highly significant cultural event in the context of a major global shift in thinking about museums as repositories and narratives of diverse cultures.

The museum community in Aotearoa, New Zealand, had an opportunity, beginning in the late 1980s, to make a major contribution to this shift in thinking by making it an integral element in the planning for its new national museum, which was opened in 1998 as the Museum of New Zealand Te Papa Tongarewa.

The Treaty of Waitangi established New Zealand as a nation in 1840. As a post-colonial society, New Zealand followed universally familiar models as its museum community grew. Despite the fact that the Treaty of Waitangi, in terms of its spirit of equality and partnership, was a historically unique agreement on shared sovereignty by an indigenous and a colonizing people, New Zealand society and its institutions, including its museums, reflected its radical proposition for nationhood more by breaching the treaty than in honoring it until late in the twentieth century. Instead, conventional colonial models of governance and social and cultural organization were established, and the indigenous Maori people of New Zealand suffered a lengthy period of physical, economic, and cultural decline that is reflected to this day.

The colonial museums of Aotearoa bore many similarities to their counterparts in other colonial cultures; by the early twentieth century, the Maori were thought of as a "dying race," while the narratives and treasures of the dominant colonial culture rapidly achieved value and recognition.

While Maori *taonga* were collected, significantly and typically in the global model, by natural history and ethnographic museums rather than history or art museums, they were not accompanied by the knowledge and belief system that animated them and gave them unique meaning. In this very basic sense, Maori *taonga*, whether in the form of physical treasures or narratives and knowledge, were treated completely differently from the artifacts, beliefs, and knowledge systems of the colonial *Pakeha* culture; they were seen as having exotic or scientific interest, but not as evidence of the unique narratives of culture and place of Aotearoa. The issue was not whether museums collected evidence of indigenous culture, but whether they collected it in the context of the knowledge and belief systems that informed indigenous evidence as an essential part of the history and ecology of this land.

The almost complete absence of recognition of *matauranga* Maori—Maori knowledge—in museums persisted until the late twentieth century. Then, a number of social and cultural threads began to come together to culminate in an extraordinary transformation—a radical repositioning of the way a post-colonial national museum could tell the stories of all its peoples and the unique place they shared.

In the early 1980s, a complex, problematic, but highly significant event took place. A multinational oil company, implicated globally in far from beneficial activities with respect to indigenous cultures and ecologies, sponsored a major exhibition of Maori carving—*Te Maori*—that toured a number of museums in the United States, including the Metropolitan Museum of Art in New York and the Field Museum in Chicago. Given the traditional placement of exhibitions of indigenous art in natural history or ethnography museums, the itinerary was in itself noteworthy. Although it is tempting to digress into an exploration of the strange discourse between culture and commerce in this project, the point that is resonant for this discussion is that *Te Maori*, in a highly intuitive, almost unplanned and inarticulate way, did bring the voice of *matauranga* Maori together with the physical treasures for the first time on a global stage.

The impact on American society and museological thinking, while highly positive, was almost certainly nowhere near as profound and enduring as was claimed at the time. What was of much more significance was the effect back in Aotearoa, in the form of growing pressure from a revived and rapidly strengthening Maori culture on the museums that held their treasures. Empowered by the positive reception of *Te Maori*, and emboldened by long overdue recognition of those unique principles of partnership in sovereignty embodied by the long dishonored Treaty of Waitangi, Iwi Maori began to assert ownership of their *taonga*. More significantly, they demanded that Maori physical culture must be seen in the context of its own knowledge and belief systems, not as artifacts under the scrutiny of Western science and subject to categorization within Western academic disciplines.

From this dynamic environment of political, social, and cultural change, Te Papa Tongarewa was born. Planning for the museum included unprecedented involvement with Iwi Maori throughout New Zealand. The involvement was, for the first time, not of a merely consultative nature, where the balance of the power in the discussion stayed firmly with the dominant culture. Instead, it moved into the much more difficult areas of ownership and empowerment within the context of a national museum. While many elements of the new museum's vision were radical, the most challenging and most successful element of its new paradigm was undoubtedly the bicultural partnership that was its strong foundation. While this integrated model and vision differ significantly from the vision for the NMAI, the challenge and opportunity offered by the recognition of First Peoples in national museums remain the same.

The bicultural partnership was the cornerstone of the development of a new model for the post-colonial national museum charged with responsibility for First Peoples' culture and history as well as settler and post-colonial migrant populations. The museum concept reflected a vision based on three organizing principles:

Tangata Whenua: People who represent the right of first discovery, the Maori.
Tangata Tiriti: People who represent the rights of the Treaty of Waitangi, the *Pakeha,* and subsequent settler groups.
Papatuanuku: The earth and environment they all share.

Although the bicultural partnership was the most challenging and controversial aspect of the museum in the eyes of the media and academic communities, not to mention Iwi themselves, the possibility of the integrated museum model rather than the development of a museum dedicated to *taonga* and *matauranga* and *tikanga* Maori was hotly debated in the planning phase. The integrated concept for the museum—bringing together collections from the historic national institutions of art, history, ethnology, and natural history—proved a radical concept from the start. Debate on the role of fine art in the context of such a museum model interestingly became implicated in the bicultural vision. Maori art was seen to fit seamlessly into such a unified concept, whereas the fine art academic community resisted—and resists to this day—any such integration of European-derived art practice into a model of narratives of culture and place.

There was a compelling acknowledgement throughout the museum—in its scholarship and research, exhibitions, events, and communications—that its founding principle was a partnership between *Pakeha* and Maori. On this foundation rests all the stories that reflect New Zealand's diversity as it becomes an increasingly multicultural nation.

Critical in achieving the paradigm shift was the development of a new approach to governance and management. A bicultural strategy was developed and accepted by the board of trustees. It embedded the partnership in a management structure that provided for a shared authority by the chief executive and *kaihautu* of the museum in all critical areas of policy and practice, not solely in aspects that involved *matauranga* and *tikanga* Maori—Maori knowledge and protocols. This ensured that as far as possible in the context of an evolving relationship, the principle of different knowledge systems as drivers for the research, display, and interpretation of material and natural culture pervaded all aspects of the museum's practice.

A further aspect of policy that would have a wide-ranging impact on the museum's entire role and responsibility for collections and knowledge was the formal agreement with Iwi Maori that the museum's collections were owned by them rather than by the museum, which became a trustee—but a trustee with the clearly articulated responsibility to adopt the appropriate approaches to *matauranga* and *tikanga* Maori and to earn the right to be a trusted custodian.

Such strategic intention was part of the vision of the museum to empower and privilege new audiences and to better reflect the nation that so richly and generously supported this very large museum project—one that is, in a sense, way out of scale with New Zealand in terms of the level of public investment. That empowerment is reflected not only in the high numbers of Maori who visit and populate the museum through Iwi exhibitions, events, and participation in the knowledge-life of the museum, but in a completely new audience for the museum as a whole—one that mirrors the makeup of New Zealand society to an unprecedented extent.

The vision that drove the Maori story was not just reflected there. The way in which the museum animates its exhibitions with the whole diversity of narratives of culture and place that make up New Zealand's story means that the empowerment of the broad audience is as effective as that for Maori audiences. The huge challenge was to understand what balance might be achieved in constructing these narratives, so that the dynamic and vibrant voice of all communities could be heard in ways that were collaborative, complementary, and inclusive, not hierarchical and exclusive.

To illustrate the process followed at Te Papa that brought this concept and vision to life, I'd like to look at four key projects that illustrate important principles of engagement with indigenous cultures and that have global implications for museums.

Ngati Hinewaka

This project is an interesting example of the intersection between Western scholarship and indigenous histories and knowledge. In the 1930s, staff of what was then called the Dominion Museum, to all intents and purposes an ethnography and natural history museum on the colonial model, conducted valuable research, albeit from an entirely Western perspective, on a Maori settlement located on the North Island, studying it from the points of view of cultural and economic development. The North Island Iwi engaged in extensive horticultural practices and trade with the South Island Iwi on a seasonal basis, retreating from their rather inhospitable coastal locations to sheltered inland valleys in winter. The early studies of the sites of these fifteenth-century dwellings formed the basis of a project for the new museum, in which knowledge acquired in the 1930s was returned to the Iwi. They, in turn, aligned it with their *matauranga* and reconstructed the *whare* buildings on their *marae* (a gathering place or place of encounter), and then in the new building. The relevant issue was the recapture of indigenous knowledge, and the return of that knowledge and its associated protocols and practices by the Iwi themselves to the new museum. All work carried out on the project was done by the Iwi.

Te Hau Ki Turanga

The same process was observed in restoring and installing the remarkable *whare nui* (carved house), *Te Hau Ki Turanga*, which was carried out by the Iwi Rongowhakaata in a lengthy process of negotiation involving the return of treasures to the Iwi's home *marae*. A complex restoration project involved rebuilding the *whare nui* as a freestanding structure in the new museum, a series of ceremonial protocols associated with the physical and spiritual transfer of the house from the old museum (again, in a physical and symbolic sense), and the development and installation by Rongowhakaata of a multimedia interpretive program inside the house.

Rongomaraeroa

Iwi Maori needed to see the museum as a *turangawaewae*, a place to stand, if the new model was to have any credibility or ownership. Accordingly, extensive negotiations over years took place between the government, the museum's development board, and Iwi Maori to lay the foundations for a unique *marae* in the museum. This *marae*, which was to be a place for all Iwi as well as all peoples of our increasingly multicultural nation, posed an enormous challenge for Maori within and outside the organization. Its vision was challenging and contemporary, and was profoundly immersed in *tikanga* and *matauranga* Maori. These forces came together in the new *marae's* extraordinary aesthetic and revolutionary practice. The project was led by the museum's *kaihautu*, Dr. Cliff Whiting, whose singular vision for Maori included a powerful recognition of the innovative nature of Maori culture and its impulse towards creative growth and engagement with the contemporary world. Given its radical conception and approach, the ownership of the *marae* from the day of its opening has been extraordinary. It rapidly became a hub for all the activities of the museum—a place of welcome for the whole nation.

The Iwi exhibition strategy emerged in tandem with this strategy for engagement and ownership. According to *tikanga,* the *marae* needed to be "warmed," populated, and spiritually charged and informed by a specific Iwi. This provided an opportunity for a series of Iwi exhibitions telling the stories and confronting the challenges and issues for Iwi throughout Aotearoa. The Iwi exhibitions, which are entirely driven in concept, narrative, and *matauranga* Maori by the Iwi, also drive the specific *tikanga,* or protocol, for *Rongomaraeroa* for the duration of the exhibition.

These examples of a transformed museum practice have ensured that the presence of indigenous peoples in an integrated museum model has been secured as a partnership reflecting shared sovereignty. This is a different model from the one we are here to celebrate, and it is one potentially fraught with risk if the major issues of the dominance of the colonial culture and the pervasiveness of Western scholarship and ownership are not addressed with courage and honesty by all stakeholders. I believe it has been shown, notably by the unprecedented ownership of Te Papa by Maori peoples, as well as by the other diverse cultures that make up New Zealand, that it is a viable model for post-colonial nations to convey their narratives of culture and place constructively and with pride as well as to acknowledge the immense spiritual and cultural conflicts and challenges that have had to be encountered along the journey.

A number of characteristics intrinsic to New Zealand society may help to explain how this transformative museum story came about. The Treaty of Waitangi is a unique founding document that was not born from conflict but from both a pragmatic and a visionary approach to the establishment of a society in which the colonizer and colonized were able to establish an agreement about shared sovereignty. The treaty is not a historic curiosity but a significant nation-building force for modern Aotearoa New Zealand It gives its museums, and especially its national museum, significant leadership roles in building a multicultural nation on powerful principles of Maori and *Pakeha* partnership.

The size, scale, and location of New Zealand are often seen as problematic for us, but in fact they have generated a kind of can-do attitude that is highly developed on our small islands. Reinvention and the development of new models that challenge norms may be related to that outlook.

New Zealand is naturally innovative and creative as a nation. While many criticized the bicultural and audience-focused model of Te Papa, they tended to reflect academic norms of Western culture rather than the intuitive value systems and strong sense of equity of the broader New Zealand populace. This is confirmed by the pattern of media response to the establishment of the museum. In the long development years, the mainstream media were unanimous and unforgiving in their expressed fear that this would become what they described as "just the Maori museum." Since the museum's opening, this concern has rarely been expressed. The museum's demographics are an exact but dynamic reflection of the demographics of the nation, and the Maori narratives and treasures are consistently revealed as the most valuable elements in the total museum experience.

While Te Papa represented a new departure for New Zealand museums, it is only one element in a global movement that has been taking place for some years now. I think of such milestones as the Museum of Civilization in Canada and the National Museum of Australia, as well as this great and historic event at which we are honored to be present. The opening of the NMAI on the National Mall is the most recent achievement of the recognition that museums can and should take unique leadership roles in their societies and communities.

It seems to me that there is no more visionary project in the context of national leadership than to restore and empower the voices of First Peoples. Here is a huge opportunity to make our nations more vibrant, dynamic, and strong. No more appropriate agencies can carry that project forward than museums, for they are unique repositories not only of the treasures but also of the narratives, knowledge, and aspirations of the world.

Kia hora te marino, kia whakapapa pounamu te moana,
Kia tere te kaarohirohi I mua I to huarahi

May peace be widespread, may the sea glisten like greenstone,
And may the shimmer of light guide you on your way.

Information desk and foyer of the Ian Potter Centre: National Gallery of Victoria, Melbourne, Australia. Photo by Predrag Cancar, NGV Photographic Services © NGV, Australia.

DES GRIFFIN

Gerard Krefft Memorial Fellow, Australian Museum, Sydney

Australian Museums and Indigenous Peoples: From Previous Possessions to Ongoing Responsibilities

I want to acknowledge the peoples and nations of this land and their elders, and those of New Zealand and Australia.[1]

The National Museum of the American Indian is among the most important of the many fine Smithsonian museums on the National Mall. It recognizes America's First Peoples. What difference will this project make? What can we learn from it?

Museums make a difference—or they can. It is shown by the crowds of interested people in the Louvre, more than in the "Grand Boulevards," by the huge numbers at the Tate Modern in London and the Metropolitan Museum in New York, by the millions at the new Ian Potter Centre: NGV Australia at Federation Square in Melbourne, and at Te Papa in Wellington, New Zealand—and not because there is nothing else to do.

It is shown by the responses of people to exhibitions such as *Darkened Waters*, on the Exxon *Valdez* oil spill, at the small Pratt Museum in Homer, Alaska, which brought to people in America the story of that event, animated by the words of those caught up in it. Fifteen years later and after a tour to seventeen venues, it is still going.[2] Another example is the exhibition *A More Perfect Union*, which opened at the Smithsonian's National Museum of American History in 1986.[3]

Internationally, economic and political rights, the right to self-determination, to education, health, housing, even happiness, are increasingly recognized. Acknowledging the universality of those rights marks us out as civilized. But those rights continue to be under threat in many countries. In dealing with museums and indigenous people, we are dealing with human rights. If there is any role more important that museums must play, it is promoting the understanding that leads to the acknowledgment by all peoples that human rights are properly rights of all peoples.

Whilst many acknowledge that to move forward we must come to terms with the past if we are genuinely to share the future, others persist in old visions and old practices. The Truth and Reconciliation Commission, achieved through the leadership of Nelson Mandela and Desmond Tutu, is not for them; nor is the planting of a cross on the reconstructed cathedral in Dresden or the commemorations, attended by German Chancellor Gerhard Schroeder, of the Normandy landings and of the 1944 Warsaw rising.

More than regrettably, one feature of history is collective inaction: nothing is done until it is too late. Conflict is a testament to failed leadership. When leaders stand back, prejudice and ignorance can bubble to the surface as people seek certainty and fail to contemplate the ambiguity that is a part of life everywhere. Ancient cultures leave us lessons to learn, but our belief in the new "New World" deflects us.

Australia and Indigenous Peoples

Australia is a federation established in 1901. First Peoples arrived more than 60,000 years ago; European colonists came in 1788. By 2004, as almost everywhere in the Western world, there have been major achievements in living standards, education, health, and economic development—but the benefits do not flow to all.

After a very few years of mostly harmonious interaction with the original inhabitants, settlers were promised free land in an "unoccupied" country, but they demanded that the government give them armed protection from the indigenous peoples whose land they cleared. Invasion, exploitation, massacres, and deaths through foreign diseases followed. People were removed to missions, recruited to pastoral properties, and taken into white homes as servants.[4] Wages—totaling perhaps a billion dollars—were often withheld.[5] Children of mixed parentage were removed forcibly from their families.[6] Today, crime, substance abuse, and imprisonment (often far from their country),[7] are typical among minorities, and statistics for health and life expectancy resemble those of people who live in developing countries.[8]

Demands by indigenous peoples for recognition in their own land began early in the nineteenth century. "The land is not merely a symbol of the political survival and identity of indigenous peoples, it is central to the worldview, the spirit and the history of all indigenous peoples in Australia. The identities, language and relationships of indigenous peoples all come from the land."[9] Lives were lost, along with much of the language, ceremony, and cultural material—but not history, not relationships, not knowledge of what happened, not a belonging to "country." Indigenous identity and culture remains proclaimed.

In 1967, after courageous lobbying by many people, a referendum overwhelmingly overturned the original provisions of the 1901 constitution. To the right of indigenous people to vote (gained in 1965) was added the right to be counted in censuses. The Australian government was also empowered to make laws for indigenous peoples.[10]

Of course, there are disagreements about the past. History is not an absolute truth. Some significant gains have been made. Some opportunities have been taken up and others passed by. Especially since 1967, centralized control was often seen as the recipe; dependence on welfare often was the response. There were also important initiatives: for instance, Cape York Partnerships address social problems through the development of a viable economy for families and communities.[11]

In 1975, the Whitlam government enacted the Racial Discrimination Act (RDA) to give effect to United Nations conventions, and introduced the Land Rights Act (ALRA), which was later passed by the Fraser government. The RDA prohibits discrimination on the basis of race at both the state and federal level. The ALRA dealt only with unalienated Crown Land.[12]

In 1991, the Australian Parliament, with bipartisan support, established a Council for Aboriginal Reconciliation. In 1992, the High Court of Australia, in the "Mabo Judgment," recognized the prior sovereignty of indigenous peoples and that continuing laws and customs accorded rights to possession and occupation of their lands. The court also accepted that to go back to an earlier time was impossible: Native title was considered extinguished where freehold title had been granted.[13]

In 1992, Prime Minister Paul Keating acknowledged, "We took the traditional lands and smashed the traditional way of life."[14] The 1993 Native Title Act created a system for Native title identification and registration. In 1996, the Wik people of northern Australia were informed by the High Court that even though pastoral leases may have been granted over their lands, Native title was not necessarily extinguished, though pastoral leases would prevail should there be inconsistency in use.[15] Conflicting claims were to be resolved through the courts or by negotiation. A new conservative government immediately passed the Native Title Amendment Act, imposing onerous tests on claims, allowing upgrading of leases for purposes other than those for which they were originally granted, restricting rights to negotiate, and so on.[16]

In 1997, at the closing ceremony of the Reconciliation Convention, some one thousand indigenous and non-indigenous people stood together. First, non-indigenous people said to indigenous people present, "We apologize for the hurt done to you, your ancestors and your lands by our ancestors and our actions over the last 209 years." Then everyone repeated the words, "Committed to walk together on this land, we commit ourselves to reconciliation and building better relationships so we can constitute a united Australia, respecting the land, valuing the Aboriginal and Torres Strait Islander heritage and providing justice and equity for all."

In 2000, hundreds of thousands of Australians walked for reconciliation. Museum people participated actively in the 1997 convention and in the walks. The Council for Reconciliation finished its term that year. The sixth and last recommendation of the council's final report was that "the Commonwealth Parliament enact legislation . . . to put in place a process which will unite all Australians by way of an agreement, or treaty, through which unresolved issues of reconciliation can be resolved."[17] No action has been taken on that.

A Change and Reorientation

For most of the first two hundred years of Australian history, museums followed the political views of the time, eagerly in many cases. The assumption was that indigenous people were going to die out and that their artifacts must be collected and displayed as curios. As indigenous people were regarded as primitive, their skulls should be measured and their bodies collected, even from graves and prisons.[18] Museums became part of the invasion and part of the oppression.

In Australia in the last thirty years, museums have sought to improve understanding and recognition of indigenous peoples. In these contested and sometimes unsafe space-times, many museums are light-years ahead of political leadership.

In 1975, the report of the Australian government inquiry into museums (the Pigott Report) proposed a Gallery of Aboriginal Australia, genuinely recognizing indigenous culture and relations with the land as major features of the proposed new national museum.[19] In 1978, questions of principles and ethics concerning indigenous cultural heritage management were addressed at *Preserving Indigenous Cultures,* a UNESCO regional seminar involving museums. In 1983, the Council of Australian Museum Directors adopted policies supporting the return of human remains and proscribing their public exhibition.

Thus by 1993, major museums in Australia had moved away from a concern with *possessions* toward a new focus on *obligations.* Holding human remains in museums was recognized as being inappropriate. Cultural material held by museums was seen to belong to those who are entitled to tell their story.[20]

Art museums—collectors of indigenous artworks from early times—continue to maintain outstanding collections of indigenous paintings, carvings, and weavings. The Museum of Contemporary Art in Sydney prominently featured traditional and contemporary works at its opening in 1991 and has acquired and holds, through a cultural partnership, complete exhibitions of material from Arnhem Land communities. The Art Gallery of New South Wales features a special large gallery of indigenous art, and so does the Ian Potter Centre: NGV Australia in Melbourne.[21]

A Policy for Museums and Indigenous Australians

In 1993, at its annual meeting, the Council of Australian Museum Associations (CAMA) launched a new policy on museums and indigenous peoples, and adopted a far-ranging resolution recognizing the rights of indigenous peoples to their culture and cultural property.[22] *Previous Possessions, New Obligations* is a comprehensive statement of principles and detailed policies. Two statements form its base:

> Different and varying interests exist in the cultural heritage of Aboriginal and Torres Strait Islander peoples. Indigenous peoples have special rights; they have primary rights. They own their intangible cultural property, the meaning of the items expressed through the design, the dance, the song, the stories.

> Australian Aboriginal and Torres Strait Islander cultures are living cultures: there are fundamental links between cultural heritage, traditional belief, and land. Rights to self-determination and basic human rights are of the greatest importance.

Following discussions in 1991 at the South Australian Museum (then the leader in relations between museums and indigenous peoples), CAMA, as the Australia-wide body representing museums of all kinds, agreed to develop relevant policy.

Participants prepared a discussion document identifying issues of perceived agreement and disagreement between museums on the one hand, and between museums and Aboriginal and Torres Strait Islander peoples on the other. Human remains, secret/sacred material, and collections in general as well as public programs, governance, and management were addressed. Past events in Australia and elsewhere as they concerned museums were recalled.

The document was circulated first to indigenous people working in museums, then more widely. Discussions, sometimes noisy, led to agreed preliminary positions by museum directors. A revised document was circulated to government and non-government museums and associations, and requests were made for consultations at the state level. Responses were incorporated and the document recirculated.

As a basis for the policy, a set of principles was drafted in mid-1992, reflecting a much stronger recognition of indigenous rights than the earlier museum directors' position. Further discussions in 1993 led to integration with a set of principles drawn up by a wholly indigenous group.

With the endorsement of the CAMA board and support from directors of major museums of all kinds and a number of Aboriginal and Torres Strait Islander organizations, the principles were launched on 18 May 1993. This was International Museum Day in the International Year for the World's Indigenous People, and it was celebrated outside Sydney's Museum of Contemporary Art at Circular Quay West, near the site of the first British settlement.

The full policy, launched seven months later, recognized the importance that human remains could have in scientific terms, but it stressed that such importance had to be established to the satisfaction of relevant people. There have been some important returns of ancient human remains.[23]

As to secret/sacred items, traditional custodians were to be consulted about disposition. Neither those items nor human remains were to be displayed. As to other collections, the policy specified that museums were to respond to *all* requests, not just those concerning items illegally acquired. The Wik decision allowed that non-indigenous interests would prevail where there was inconsistency, but this policy instead provided that indigenous interests would prevail.

Previous Possessions, New Obligations made clear that all public programming should involve the relevant Aboriginal and Torres Strait Islander community members. Although it could take longer to plan public programs, it was agreed that excluding indigenous communities would continue unsatisfactory practices of representation without consultation and knowledge. The policy also emphasized the appointment, training, and involvement of indigenous staff and indigenous representation on boards and committees.

In 1994, a committee under the auspices of the Australian government was established to advise on government-funded programs concerning return, and a program was established in 1998.[24] As we transited to the next century, however, problems remained, including government attitudes, the level of commitment (particularly among smaller museums), and the issue of whether indigenous people themselves saw the policy as a basis for their own action.[25] Museums Australia is revising the policy document under the title *Continuous Cultures, Ongoing Responsibilities* to take into account the findings of a review conducted in 2000.[26]

Toward Ongoing Obligations: Museums in Australia Now

The situation in Australia resembles developments in other countries. In the United States, the Native American Graves Protection and Repatriation Act was enacted in 1989. Changes in practice are most noticeable in areas mandated by the legislation; museums consider control over process and achieving direct and tangible benefit to be important.[27] In Canada, *Turning the Page: Forging New Relationships Between Museums and First Peoples* was developed by the Canadian Museums Association and First Nations in 1992, but reductions in museum funding have impeded progress and placed the onus for action on museums.[28]

Australian museums, mainly the larger ones, have successfully implemented sensitive management of collections of human remains[29] and secret/sacred material, and have included indigenous people and indigenous perspectives in public programs. New issues, including availability of resources in outlying regions, have emerged. Museums and communities often compete for funding; support for research by indigenous people is needed.[30] Recent events show progress. In 2003, some eight hundred items, including secret/sacred material and human remains from collections of all major state museums, were returned to people of the Pilbara area in northwestern Australia. Museum Victoria has returned more than seven hundred ancestral remains in the last few years. The small but important Macleay Museum at the University of Sydney has returned human remains to communities across Australia. Over the last fifteen years, the Queensland Museum has returned 155 of their pre-1990 holdings of 635 remains and twenty-seven of the 278 sacred objects. Ownership of a further eighty-two remains and forty-three objects has been transferred to indigenous communities.[31]

What a contrast this progress is in Australia, Canada, and the United States. At the American Association of Museums conference in 1989, a senior Onondaga chief told of Cree warriors running from the Canadian plains through the snow all the way to the American Museum of Natural History in New York to seek return of an important medicine bundle, only to be told that the museum had bought it and thus owned it.

Now in Australia, at cultural gatherings, exhibition openings, and book launches, indigenous people are recognized, guests are welcomed to "country" by indigenous people, and speakers acknowledge Native people and their lands. There is an active interface between major museums and indigenous peoples covering employment and governance. National parks authorities similarly pay attention to former indigenous occupation and lifeways in their interpretative labeling.

Four state museums and the national museum have opened important exhibitions recognizing indigenous peoples, their culture, and their history in the last ten years. Most deal with conflict since 1788, the removal of children, and deaths in custody. Living indigenous people are depicted. The Australian Museum's *Indigenous Australians* exhibition commenced, as in other museums, with intensive consultation with indigenous and non-indigenous Australians.

All this has meant conceptual shifts from historical representations to contemporary ones, from museum interpretations to indigenous peoples' stories of their own experiences, from object-focused to thematic exhibitions.[32] Interviews with visitors reveal they are willing to listen to and explore contemporary issues. Visitors to the Australian Museum's exhibition, prompted by photographs, wrote vivid descriptions of how they remembered feeling at particular times in the exhibition. Similar findings emerge from studies of visitors at other recently opened exhibitions.[33] Many had been unaware in any detail of past histories and the depth and richness of indigenous cultures, and they appreciated learning of that.

Notwithstanding these positive responses, the National Museum of Australia's *First Australians* exhibition was criticized by people who held more conventional views of what history is, what truth is, and what museums should be. Some objected to the emphasis on oral history and the focus on massacres.[34]

A New Century—A New Opportunity?

Four years into this century, the demands of many in Australia for recognition of indigenous history and present life go unheard by the government. A country once admired for progress in social justice—a country known as much for the claim on a "fair go" as for its prowess in cricket, the Americas Cup (once), shrimps on the "barby," its films, music, and other cultural attainments—has stumbled. There are those who question their identity as Australians.

In the 2003 Australia Day address, Rick Farley, former executive director of the National Farmers' Federation and a member of the Council for Aboriginal Reconciliation, observed, "The Native Title Act has not served its purpose . . . recognition and protection of native title [has not been achieved]. Instead, it has become a mechanism to constrain and extinguish native title. It has not delivered a just compromise for Aboriginal people, whose position in our society has not improved. . . . The transaction costs are enormous. There has to be a better way."

At the May 2004 Sydney Writers Festival, historian Inga Clendinnen, an expert on the Aztec peoples of North and Central America, spoke of the first years of contact between the English and indigenous people at Sydney Cove, of how, in accordance with instructions from the British government, Governor Phillip exercised patience and leadership in respecting Aboriginal people, and of how later, when settlers came—"very hard men indeed"— violent and bloody conflicts flared up. To a large extent it was over different concepts of law.[35] Clendinnen concluded:

> We are still struggling with sculpting a delicate interface between Aboriginal understandings of law where we have still got functioning communities with such understandings which are different from ours, and the law of the dominant culture. . . . It is only if each group acknowledges the possibility of justice achieved within each system that we can hope for any kind of viable rec-

onciliation. . . . However I have to say right now, that [certain actions] of the Federal Government . . . rip away that delicate, informed-by-experience system of particular accommodations which could make justice through law a viable possibility. We are back with Phillip now!

How Do Museums Make a Difference?

In considering the impact of this wonderful new museum, we should ask, "How do museums make a difference, and what do such museums look and feel like?" Unless we have in place the social processes that are necessary to allow various professional skills to be applied, the museum will not succeed in the community, and the knowledge and skills of the staff will be irrelevant or wasted on the organization. It requires patience, understanding, trust, and commitment to the sharing of information and cooperation to get people to seek a common vision of the future.[36]

In the development of the National Museum of the American Indian, leadership has never wavered from the vision and the goal, and has never been deflected by the difficulties that plague all projects from creating a cohesive and can-do culture. At the NMAI, understanding and acknowledging past history—and building trust with and respecting the Native peoples who have an absolute interest in the management, interpretation, and disposition of collections—are central concerns, notwithstanding the size of the collections and the structural and cultural complexities.[37] I have heard of the clear, shared understanding of purpose among staff working with, talking about, and reflecting on Native peoples and the living cultures this museum is to honor and celebrate.[38] Values are clear, ceremonies are enacted when necessary, and those who exercise leadership are those who are appropriate to the occasion.

Much of current political and religious discourse is no more than rhetoric, backward-looking, self-serving, inflexible, seemingly unchallengeable, even dishonest. We need genuine leadership. When we see it, we should understand it and emulate it. That is what the NMAI can significantly contribute.

Notwithstanding neoliberal economics, managerialism, concern with the short-term, and often a failure to seek out the truth, I expect that many museums will continue to promote understanding of our culturally diverse humanity. We will have to take a much broader and more active role if we are to go beyond rhetoric in addressing inequities and prejudice. Indigenous wisdom, not least because of its great age, has much to contribute.

Museums are often cast as being about the past, but they can be about the future as well. Only by addressing the fears and respecting the aspirations of others, by celebrating our common humanity, can we live together.

Acknowledgments

I especially thank Tim Sullivan and Peter Hiscock (both of Sovereign Hill Museums Association, Ballarat), Lori Richardson (Department of Communications, Information Technology and the Arts, Canberra), and Janette Griffin (University of Technology, Sydney) for their critical reading of the manuscript. Meredith Hinchliff and Lorraine Fitzpatrick (Museums Australia), Carl Bento, Phil Gordon, Peter White and Lynda Kelly (Australian Museum), Susan Tonkin (National Museum of Australia), Michael Green and Carolyn Meehan (Melbourne Museum), Mance Lofgren (Western Australian Museum), and Ian Galloway (Queensland Museum) assisted with information on policies, programs, visitors, and images.

1. Although I speak of indigenous peoples, I do not speak *for* them nor do I seek to represent their views.

2. Mike O'Meara, "Let the People Speak," *Journal of Museum Education* 28, no. 3 (2003), 9–12.

3. *A More Perfect Union* explored the experiences of Americans of Japanese ancestry during World War II. The exhibition is online at http://americanhistory.si.edu/perfectunion/experience/index.html.

4. The full text of the five lectures that make up the Vincent Lingiari Memorial Lectures (1996–2000)—which were presented by distinguished Australians, including two senior indigenous people, a governor-general, and two former prime ministers—can be found at http://www.curriculumsupport.nsw.edu.au/hsie/speak/pages/invaevid.htm.

5. Information on this is available at a number of sites, including that of Australians for Native Title and Reconciliation (http://antar.dovenetq.net.au/03_news/mrnat080803.pdf).

6. The "Report of the National Inquiry into the Separation of Aboriginal and Torres Strait Islander Children from Their Families," published in 1997, is at http://www.austlii.edu.au/au/special/rsjproject/rsjlibrary/hreoc/stolen/.

7. The "Report of the Royal Commission on Aboriginal Deaths in Custody," published in 1991, is at http://www.austlii.edu.au/au/special/rsjproject/rsjlibrary/rciadic/.

8. Statistics are at the Australian Bureau of Statistics website, http://www.abs.gov.au. Information is also available from the Australian Institute of Health and Welfare

(http://www.aihw.gov.au/publications/index.cfm/title/9226).

9. See Lisa Strelein in collaboration with First Peoples Worldwide, "Aboriginal Land Rights in Australia," available at http://www.firstpeoples.org/land_rights/australia/land_rights_in_australia.htm.

10. The words "other than the aboriginal people in any State" were removed from section 51 (xxvi) of the Constitution: "The Parliament shall, subject to this Constitution, have power to make laws for the peace, order, and good government of the Commonwealth with respect to the people of any race [words deleted] for whom it is necessary to make special laws."

11. See http://www.capeyorkpartnerships.com/.

12. See Strelein, "Aboriginal Land Rights."

13. Details of the Mabo Judgment of the High Court can be found at http://www.austlii.edu.au/au/special/rsjproject/rsjlibrary/archives/mabo/; also http://home.vicnet.net.au/~aar/aarmabo.htm.

14. Speaking at Redfern Park in Sydney on December 10, 1992, Keating said, "We cannot sweep injustice aside. . . . Australia once reached out for us. Didn't Australia provide opportunity and care for the dispossessed Irish? The poor of Britain? The refugees from war and famine and persecution in the countries of Europe and Asia? Surely we can find just solutions to the problems which beset the first Australians—the people to whom the most injustice has been done. . . . The problem starts with us non-Aboriginal Australians. It begins, I think, with the act of recognition. Recognition that it was we who . . . failed to see that what we were doing degraded all of us."

15. A comprehensive account of the Wik Judgment of the High Court can be found at http://www.isis.aust.com/wik/.

16. A summary of the Howard government's "Ten Point Plan," which formed the basis of the Native Title Amendment Act of 1997, is provided by the Human Rights and Equal Opportunity Commission's Aboriginal and Torres Strait Islander Social Justice Commissioner at http://www.austlii.edu.au/au/other/IndigLRes/1997/4/7.html.

17. The report, *Reconciliation: Australia's Challenge*, presented to the prime minister of Australia on December 4, 2000, can be found at http://www.austlii.edu.au/au/other/IndigLRes/car/2000/16/dkblueintro01.htm. The speech by Dr. Mick Dodson (first Aboriginal and Torres Strait Islander Social Justice Commissioner in the Human Rights and Equal Opportunity Commission) at the celebrations of the Fifth National Reconciliation Week—"Corroboree 2000"—in May 2000 is at http://www.austlii.edu.au/au/orgs/car/media/Dr%20Mick%20Dodson.htm.

18. Consider this statement: "Skeletons of Aborigines are much wanted . . . authentic skulls may be obtained from the graves of the natives of each tribe." It is included in *Hints for the preservation of specimens of natural history*, published by the Australian Museum, Sydney, in 1887. (See the Australian Museum's website http://deathonline.net/disposal/preservation/exhibiting.cfm).

19. P. Pigott et al., *Museums in Australia, 1975* (Canberra: AGPS, 1975).

20. For an account of Australian Museum actions, see Jim Specht and Carolyn MacLulich, "Challenges and Changes: The Australian Museum and Indigenous Communities," in *Archae-*

ological Displays and the Public: Museology and Interpretation, 2nd ed., Paulette M. McManus, ed. (London: Archetype Publications, 2000), 39–63.

21. Susan Cochrane, ed. *Aboriginal Art Collections: Highlights from Australia's Public Museums and Galleries* (Sydney: Craftsman House, 2001). The Museum of Contemporary Art cultural partnership was negotiated under the leadership of then Chief Curator Bernice Murphy. See Djon Mundine, *The Native Born: Objects and Representations from Ramingining, Arnhem Land* (Sydney: Museum of Contemporary Art, 1996).

22. The resolution recognized Australian Aboriginal and Torres Strait Islander peoples as the original inhabitants and owners of the lands and as having unique, distinctive, and different cultural traditions from all of those peoples who arrived subsequently in Australia. They were also recognized as having primary and inalienable rights of ownership of their cultural property, its interpretation, transmission, and continued development. The resolution urged they be accorded this unique and primary position in all statements of cultural policy development in Australia.

23. Some of the remains—of considerable and much debated age—found at Lake Mungo in southwestern New South Wales and Kow Swamp in northern Victoria have been returned to relevant Aboriginal communities. The Vermillion Accord, adopted by the World Archaeological Congress in August 1989, emphasized that "respect for the dead shall be accorded to all irrespective of origin, race, religion, nationality, custom and tradition and that wishes of the dead concerning disposition shall be abided by wherever possible, so shall the wishes of the local community . . ." There is no Australian government policy on the return of remains.

24. The "Return of Indigenous Cultural Property Scheme," an initiative of the Cultural Ministers' Council managed by the Australian government's Department of Communications, Information Technology and the Arts, is described at http://www.dcita.gov.au/Article/0,,0_1-2_2-3_478-4_103542,00.html.

25. D. J. G. Griffin, "Previous Possessions, New Obligations: A Commitment by Australian Museums," *Curator* 39, no. 1 (1996), 45–62; also
see http://www.desgriffin.com/publications/reconciliation.htm.

26. The Museums Australia website and links are at http://www.museumsaustralia.org.au./hot-topics.htm.

27. T. J. Sullivan, M. Abraham, and D. J. G. Griffin, "NAGPRA, Effective Repatriation Programs and Cultural Change in Museums," *Curator* 43, no. 3 (2001), 231–60.

28. Michael M. Ames, "Are Changing Representations of First Peoples in Canadian Museums and Galleries Challenging the Curatorial Prerogative?" in *The Changing Presentation of the American Indian: Museums and Native Cultures* (Washington, D.C.: National Museum of the American Indian, Smithsonian Institution, in association with University of Washington Press, Seattle, 2000), 73–88.

29. The present attitude is exemplified by the inclusion of the following statement on the Australian Museum's website (http://deathonline.net/disposal/preservation/exhibiting.cfm), which contrasts with the notice of 117 years ago (see note 18 above): "Indigenous laws hold that the deceased will not enjoy spiritual rest until they are returned to their ancestral home and given the last rites in accordance with tradition." Aboriginal and Torres Strait Islander

Social Justice Commissioner, as quoted in "Our Culture: Our Future," *Report on Australian Indigenous Cultural and Intellectual Property Rights* (1998).

30. Tim Sullivan, Lynda Kelly, and Phil Gordon, "Museums and Indigenous People in Australia: A Review of *Previous Possessions, New Obligations*," *Curator* 46, no. 2 (2003), 208–27.

31. Most of these returns have occurred since 2000 under the "Return of Indigenous Cultural Property Program." The museum now recognizes that indigenous knowledge lies with communities. The museum is now facilitator, not expert—custodian, not owner. A new Aboriginal and Torres Strait Islander Cultural Centre is due to open at the Museum's South Bank site in December 2005. Ian Galloway, personal communication.

32. L. Kelly and P. Gordon, "Developing a Community of Practice: Museums and Reconciliation in Australia," in *Museums, Society, Inequality*, R. Sandell, ed. (London: Routledge, 2002), 153–74.

33. An independent consultant's report on the Melbourne Museum's exhibition, *Bunjilaka*, found it to be "predominantly a cultural, personal and sometimes emotional experience and absorbing for visitors," and that it provided "an opportunity to learn and experience Aboriginal culture and history." Carolyn Meehan, personal communication, August 6, 2004.

34. When asked what were the main things they liked about the National Museum of Australia, visitors frequently mentioned the *First Australians* Gallery. When asked for specific comments, indigenous people talked of being impressed by "lots of good things," "It's good they keep our things in there. . . ." Non-indigenous people said, "Very impressive; changed our views," "Excellent, comprehensive. Too much to take in at one visit. . . ." and "Extremely moving—information beautifully handled, wears its scholarship lightly." A minority of visitors described the exhibition as "a shameless propaganda exercise" and suggested Aboriginal people should just stop whingeing. Susan Tonkin, personal communication, July 28, 2004. A formal review (*A Report to the Council of the National Museum of Australia, July 2003*) found that "the Museum presented with some success the history of the Indigenous peoples in the *Gallery of First Australians* . . . [and] has rightly earned the praise of the general public, and of academic and museum specialists." One media article said, "[The Report] made no finding of systematic political bias, declaring only that some of the exhibits might be open to misinterpretation." See *The Age*, Melbourne, December 15, 2003.

35. See ABC Radio National website for the "Hindsight" program, http://www.abc.net.au/rn/history/hindsight/stories/s1133457.htm.

36. D. J. G. Griffin, "Managing in the Museum Organisation I. Leadership and Communication," *International Journal of Museum Management and Curatorship* 6 (1987), 387–98; D. J. G. Griffin, "Managing in the Museum Organisation II. Conflict, Tasks, Responsibilities," *International Journal of Museum Management and Curatorship* 7 (1988), 11–23.

37. James Pepper Henry, "Challenges in Maintaining Culturally Sensitive Collections at the National Museum of the American Indian," in Lawrence E. Sullivan and Alison Edwards, eds. *Stewards of the Sacred* (Washington, D.C.: American Association of Museums, in cooperation with the Center for the Study of World Religions, Harvard University, 2004).

38. Tim Sullivan, personal communication.

Guns and Bibles displayed in the National Museum of the American Indian exhibition, *Our Peoples: Giving Voice to Our Histories*. Photos by Katherine Fogden (Mohawk). © NMAI.

RICHARD W. HILL SR.

Teacher, Artist, and Museum Consultant
Former Assistant Director for Public Programs, NMAI

IN SEARCH OF AN INDIGENOUS PLACE: MUSEUMS AND INDIGENOUS CULTURE

IN HIS ESSAY "SELLING NATIONS: INTERNATIONAL EXHIBITIONS AND CULTURAL DIPLOMACY," Brian Wallis tells of a $10 million campaign to promote Mexico in New York City in 1990. The theme of that campaign was "Mexico: A Work of Art."[1] Wallis considered this campaign troublesome because it "alludes to the invented nature of nationality and to the role of culture in defining the nation to natives and foreigners alike." By promoting a country as a work of art, we might miss the underlying culture as well as the social realities faced by that nation. In many ways, the National Museum of the American Indian is being promoted as a work of art. It is promoted as an indigenous place where art shines. Do we run the danger of not being able to see the forest of indigenous realities for the art trees?

Wallis notes that we have come to understand that "identity is often constructed through cultural representations." This is certainly true for indigenous identities. Using art as a form of cultural diplomacy, according to Wallis, can result in several social changes: a distortion of history, a commercialization of culture, a breaking of stereotypes, or a breakthrough in constructive cross-cultural relationships. By cultural diplomacy, Wallis is referring to the marketing of a culture for social, political, and economic gains. While many might hate to admit it, this is also happening in the indigenous world.

Further, Wallis argues that the negatives of this kind of cultural diplomacy do not outweigh the positives. He states that such approaches only create "encapsulated, easily digestible vignettes" of a foreign culture, yet "scarcely broach the complicated issues raided by any contemporary, multicultural society or touch on the contradictions or conflicts in the histories of the countries they represent." This gets to the heart of the matter. If we see the National Museum of the American Indian as a form of cultural diplomacy, then we realize that the deeper substance of cultural expression might get lost to the vignettes of the living arts.

In 1990, I was the director of the Institute of American Indian Arts Museum in Santa Fe, New Mexico, and we were promoting our new museum with the theme "Indian Art Through Indian Eyes." Our goal was to present Native American art on its own terms, as reflected by the collections of a federally chartered art school for Indians. Our assumption was that art meant something different to Indians than it does to other cultures. We were trying to get the art elite of America to consider our art as fine art, deserving of a place in the major cultural centers of the museum world. In many ways, as indigenous curators, we have been caught in the trap described by Wallis. The objectives of our representations of indigenous art have been focused on social and political goals as much as they have been on aesthetic issues. The irony of it all finally got to me. As Indians were rushing to get their work in mainstream museums, the Smithsonian was building a museum to house our art separately from other cultures. Who was right?

What Is Indigenous Art?

I have been asked to start a conversation about "indigenous art." What is it? How does it fit into existing non-indigenous models of representation and interpretation? How does it not? And how do all of the above affect what museums do in looking at and presenting exhibitions and public programs of "indigenous art?"

The first step is to define the parameters of what indigenous art and culture means from an indigenous perspective. I used to argue that indigenous art and culture can be measured by its content and intent. In my mind, our arts and cultures had to be about certain things from our inherited worlds, aimed at our relatives in order to keep the ideals of those inherited worlds alive for at least one more generation. To me, art and culture are part of the performance of daily life, not an end product intended for the museum audience. Similarly, both art and culture had to exist in an indigenous space in order to be fully functional. I saw indigenous art as the ability to live a creative way of life, no matter what the circumstances of that life. Therefore, indigenous art is the way in which we manifest this creative way of life. I was in denial, in that some of the art is actually made for the museum culture, not the local culture. I could not fit all of the indigenous art into my theoretical framework.

I therefore sought to "indigenize" the museum space through my curatorial work, to create a new atmosphere of appreciation, and have the style of representation be reflective of the cultural/art values of the cultures represented. Certainly the consultations I conducted with Native Americans when I worked at the NMAI encouraged me to think that it was possible on a national scale. I was captivated by the enthusiasm of the Native people across the country in defining the kind of space they wanted on the Mall. In fact, the Native artists created the most exciting vision of what this space could do. The results of these consultations are described in *The Way of the People*. That unpublished report, however, does not capture the hope and strength I witnessed as people created the museum space in their minds.

As time passed I began to wonder if any museum could be that kind of space, where that creative way of life can be lived. If the primary purpose of a museum is to share the art and culture with nonbelievers, I had my doubts. I grew increasingly disheartened by the elements of cultural diplomacy (as described by Wallis) that I saw time and again in museum planning. Museums were attempting to be social engineers, capitalizing on the popularity of Native culture and art, but they were always confused about the art and cultures that they attempted to represent. In fact, museums may have a stifling effect on the vitality of indigenous life because of the need to minimize the expression of the culture to fit the needs of the museum.

Museums' Manifest Destiny

"Our way lies, not over trampled nations, but through desert wastes, to be brought by our industry and energy within the domain of art and civilization," stated John L. O'Sullivan, editor of the *New York Morning News*, when he wrote about Manifest Destiny on October 13, 1845. "We are contiguous to a vast portion of the globe, untrodden save by the savage and the beast, and we are conscious of our power to render it tributary to man. . . . With the valleys of the Rocky Mountains covered into pastures and sheep-folds, we may with propriety turn to the world and ask, 'Whom have we injured?'"

The premise that the natural world can be reconstituted to fit the "domain of art and civilization" is a unifying value of museums in America, perhaps the world. The "savage" and the beast were to be made "tributary" to the dominant society, which developed sciences to define, describe, and analyze the indigenous peoples of the world. In the early stages of these sciences, racial overtones and cultural biases painted a bleak representation of indigenous culture and art. *Whom* have we injured? Everyone.

Museums were erected to manifest attitudes of cultural and racial superiority. The harsh reality is that much of what was collected from Indians came as a result of war booty, illicit trade, and outright theft and duplicity. The indigenous peoples of the Americas were seen as a sacrificial race on the altar of expansionism. This trade in cultural patrimony has left an enduring scar upon the cultural landscape. It is what repatriation is all about.

Fortunately, we have moved way beyond those early days of institutional racism. Museums have remade themselves in light of new social realities. Yet, Wallis's words of the "encapsulated, easily digestible vignettes" still ring through my head when I walk through museum exhibitions. Despite the changes within, museums generally represent places of "truth" to the visitor, places where you can see real objects and hear from real scholars. People come to have their sense of the truth reaffirmed or to gain some new insight into some commonly held ideas of life, culture, or art.

Museums have the power to manipulate our sense of self, our collective identity, our sense of the past, and our vision of the future. I say manipulation because museum representations have become more driven by physiological and sociological factors employed by museum planners, exhibit designers, and museum educators. This is not necessarily a bad thing. Our museum experiences have become more intuitive, more connected to all of the senses, and we absorb ideas rather than be told what to think. In critiquing the impact of this new style of museology, we must consider who is manipulating the sense of destiny that we will absorb about indigenous peoples. What is the worldview that drives the museum experience of today? Is it an indigenous worldview?

The Only Good Indian Art is Dead Indian Art

The story of Little Finger Nail, a Northern Cheyenne warrior-artist may help us understand museum representation. Little Finger Nail made drawings in a ledger book that he carried during the last few months of his life. He was held captive at Fort Robinson, Nebraska, in 1878 and 1879. His drawings were a narrative of the time when the Cheyennes under Dull Knife had surrendered and were forced from their reservation in Indian Territory to their former homelands in Wyoming Territory. His art is as much a historical document as it is a visual expression of his life.

Francis Hardie was the post adjutant who had tried to purchase the ledger book from the warrior-artist several times. Little Finger Nail always refused to part with it. Hardie wrote that when the Cheyenne broke out of their confinement, he sent troopers to stop them. As it turned out, sixty-four of the 149 Cheyenne prisoners were killed—men, women, and children alike.

Little Finger Nail was among those killed. A bullet tore through that book of memories. The artist's blood mixed with the images of his life. Prior to the shooting, Hardie had seen Little Finger Nail place the ledger book in his waist belt.

"When the fight was over, and as the dead Indians were being pulled out of the rifle pit, they drew out finally my Indian with the book, apparently dead; the book was injured to the extent of a carbine ball through it and was more or less covered with fresh blood," Hardie recalled. He picked up the book from Little Finger Nail's dead body and decided to keep it. Hardie finally got his wish.

Eventually, the ledger book changed hands and made its way to the American Museum of Natural History in New York City. When I saw the actual book and later learned of the story, I could not think about if it was fine art or not. I could not think about how best to display it to show the artistry at work; nor could I understand how this visual diary taken off a dead man could be ethically used to explain Cheyenne culture. He should have been buried with it, or it should have been given to his relatives to decide its fate. The fact that the artist died trying to keep both the ledger and his way of life safe made me angry.

From a museum point of view, the ledger book has several narratives. First, there is the story of how the warriors came to carry such books. Next, there are the actual stories represented by the drawings. Then, there is the story of how the Cheyenne came to be imprisoned in Nebraska. Finally, there is the story of how the ledger book ended up in the American Museum of Natural History. All of these are the types of Native narratives behind Indian art. Yet, not all the stories can be presented in the museum. Given the details of this story, is the quality of the art even an issue in the real meaning of the drawings? The main question is: Why did Little Finger Nail have to die? That story could be told without the ledger book. It seldom is.

It's Indigenous, But Is It Art?

Edmund Carpenter was a scholar and a former trustee of the Museum of the American Indian. He believed that, to Western culture, art is public property, but for Indians, it often has private purposes. Many Native objects, according to Carpenter, were not meant to be seen by everyone. He called these works the "silent music" and "hidden art" that exist within the members of the Native society. By showing those types of objects in a museum, can the viewer hear that silent music?

For about one hundred years, curators have argued about how much background information is necessary to appreciate the artistic significance of indigenous art. Without the social, cultural, historical, and personal narratives, can we still appreciate the imagery on a purely visual level? Does knowing the artist died seeking freedom in his own land enhance the meaning of the art described above?

Native narratives are the stories and visual accounts of events that have shaped our collective identity as indigenous people in modern society. Whether true or fictitious, these narratives have become the oral history and shared memory of our generations. This kind of oral history becomes part of our culture, a part that is seldom shared in public spaces, in part, because it is too painful. The wounds of the past are still festering. We keep these stories to ourselves, in large part because everything else has been stripped away. There are some vital stories that we need to keep to ourselves, just as there are sacred ceremonies that are not meant for public display. Without these essential stories and ways of expression, it is difficult for a museum to describe what drives the hearts and souls of a culture. We get a small sliver of the reality. By only looking at the veneer of a tree, we do not see the growth rings inside.

There must be artistic territory in which the art made by indigenous artists exists in its own right. We are not the "Outsiders" because we follow a different system of beliefs. We are not the "Other" defined in reaction to accepted norms of the mainstream. We are our own norm. We are not the "Fourth World," measured against the white First World, because economic hierarchy is no measure of cultural substance. We are the indigenous artists who make expressions of our realities. Our realities belong to us, not in a museum.

Few museums collected the everyday things Native Americans used during the era of transformation from being a free people to being a reservation culture. Plain clothing was overlooked in the search for ritual "costumes." Decorative crafts were preferred over survival crafts. Only those items that connected to an older tradition were considered authentic. It is telling that Indian beadwork and dance outfits made after 1900 were seldom collected by the major museums. Anything else was not considered authentic. There is little or no material that discussed assimilation, relocation, termination, or self-determination, despite the fact that these major federal policies affected at least three-quarters of the Indians in this country. The politics of Indian realities was edited out, either by the artist, the Indian agent, the collector, or the curator.

As a result, we are forced to try and tell our stories by what was collected. It is an incomplete picture. We are faced with the impossible task of describing the metaphysics of our universe in one hundred and fifty words or less. We must explain our philosophies and histories at a sixth-grade level of comprehension. These are the reasons why museum exhibitions seem to trivialize our stories. It is not done purposefully in order to demean our stories; it is the result of a very limited process of interpretation.

The Way of the People

In *The Way of the People*, the founding document that defines the scope of interpretation for the NMAI, Santa Clara Pueblo architect Rina Swentzell suggests that indigenous societies share some common principles, which are essential in the representation and interpretation of our respective ways of being. As Swentzell sees it, representation and interpretation should include issues of interrelationships to the land and the people. They should reflect the cycles of the organic world, the natural continuum of which we are all a part, and understandings of the reciprocal nature of the universe, where respect and sharing are the driving values. Ultimately, in the Swentzell view of interpretation and representation, it is about understanding and exercising our responsibilities and obligations to the cycle of life.

While a museum can present and discuss aspects of that cycle of life, there is no consequence for the museum if that way of life is not practiced within. Museum visitors cannot exercise their responsibility to the cycle of life by spending forty-five minutes looking at objects in glass cases. The museum and its exhibitions, however, can stimulate reflective thinking on these matters. This was the challenge faced by the Native architects and planners of the NMAI. Could they mimic the natural continuum in a constructed space without making it too culturally specific?

We will judge their accomplishments differently as we can now stand in the museum space. Our responses will be shaped by how well we ourselves understand and live with those connects described by Swentzell. To me, the real issue is the power of belief. That is what makes our lives, our communities, and our art unique. It is our unique belief systems working within communities and specialized environments that make our cultures work. Indigenous societies do share commonalities and some universal attitudes. I have come to realize, however, the importance of place, family, and community as the essential elements in making the complete indigenous person. It is the relationships to place, family, and community, combined with the spiritual beliefs of our ancestors, that create the pattern for our own way of being. It is a path that leads us to a journey of creativity as we explore new ways to manifest those old realities.

No museum can replicate these essential relationships because a museum is not an avenue to the power of belief. Museums can respect the fact that those beliefs exist and try to interpret the significance of those beliefs, but a strange sense of disconnect results. Instead, we try to look at the objects of identity and belief as art and often cannot imagine their real significance unless we are practitioners of the belief behind those objects.

Native Place or Not?

I was both impressed and depressed by a sign outside the new museum that was welcoming me to an Indian place. My first reaction was, "No, you are wrong. This is not an Indian place. It is a federal facility." Native people do not govern this place; it is an instrumentality of the Smithsonian. This became even clearer when I was denied entrance by an African American security guard. That does not happen in too many Indian places that I have visited. After all the planning about entering from the east, I was forced to enter from the south for security reasons. My first experience with the building did not fulfill the mandate defined in *The Way of the People*.

"The museum is propelled by a social and moral consciousness," states *The Way of the People*. "It is an instrument of social change addressing and reaching beyond misconceptions and stereotypes of Native American cultures and peoples." This would imply that the museum has a social and moral obligation. Think of Wallis's notion of cultural diplomacy. Beyond the standard role of education, the NMAI gave itself a special role as the instrument of change. We need to be clear about whose social and moral consciousness it represents: that of the indigenous people or the federal government's? These two consciousnesses have clashed in the past. The NMAI is part of a federal agency and has its own legal mandate (federal interest), its board mandates (social interests), and staff mandates to "give voice" to Native America. We already have a voice. The museum becomes the editor of our voices.

Time will tell if the NMAI is able to manifest the mandate expressed in *The Way of the People* AND create a space where the indigenous people manifest their own representations, without editorial oversight. I suggest that the curators go back and read that massive document and then assess their own work according to those standards.

Living Within the Indian Congress

Is an Indian-owned casino an indigenous place? How about a Catholic church on the reservation with Indian murals painted on the walls? Or a nuclear waste repository designed by an Indian architect? Different belief systems drive each of these places, yet the same people may experience them. The social, cultural, and spiritual environments can sometimes transcend the physical setting in which indigenous people find themselves. I would like to think that indigenous expression is strong enough to exist anywhere, yet we think of the natural world when we think of authentic indigenous spaces.

In the nineteenth century, cultural expositions became very popular. Indigenous peoples were featured in many of these early world's fairs. Inspired by the model of the Wild West Show, Indians were presented in what became known as the Indian Congress, an intertribal gathering of cultural performers.

In 1892, America wanted to celebrate the world that was created after the arrival of Christopher Columbus. One year later, the World's Columbian Exposition opened in Chicago. Representations of Native Americans were part of that exposition. The Indian Congress was defined in the Columbian promotional literature as the place where "the different tribes of Indians appear before the visitor, presenting their different styles of war and ghost dances, with their songs and weird musical accompaniments. Seats are arranged in a semi-circle in the center of which the performance is conducted."[2]

The brochures also declared that the Indian Congress would provide "picturesque and impressive" views of the "primitive Indian" by showing "baskets, blankets, jewelry, bead work, pottery, etc." Is material culture the right lens through which to interpret indigenous philosophy and belief? What ten objects would you pick to describe the defining moments of your personal history, the underlying values of your belief systems, and your deeply held cultural-political-social convictions? In this regard, the arts are only part of the story.

Also in 1893, noted historian Frederick Jackson Turner declared that the frontier was a meeting point between the realms of savagery and civilization. Expositions safely transported people to those "savage" peoples and places. Turner suggested that the American pioneers had to assume the role of the Indian on the frontier because the frontier "environment is at first too strong for the man. He must accept the conditions which it furnishes, or perish, and so he fits himself into the Indian clearing and follows the Indian trails." Perhaps this is the reason why some in the United States began to look at Native Americans as a "vanishing American" and sought so diligently to capture the fleeting memories of culture through fine art, literature, movies, and popular culture.

Museums began by making the "savage" world safe for civilized gazing. By looking at Native cultures, Americans sought a part of themselves to reflect upon the savagery of their own past actions. They also wanted to be able to visualize the future of their more advanced civilization that resulted from those past actions. This made for a very interesting kind of reflection.

In 1996, the Institutional Studies Office of the Smithsonian conducted a visitor opinion survey of the new National Museum of the American Indian in New York City, more commonly referred to as the Heye Center. That survey produced the following opinions about Native Americans:

1) The visitor had a strong sense that Native Americans are different from other Americans. The visitor noted that the difference can be a source of learning.

2) The visitor wanted an emphasis on Native American attitudes toward

nature. The visitor sought to understand cultural differences in relationship to views of the universe. The visitor had a deep awareness that such relationships can be seen in the arts.

3) The visitor felt a strong sense of the cycle of life in looking at Native art and culture.

4) The visitor felt that images in the media are quite different from the holistic image. The casino image seems to conflict with traditional values of Native Americans. The visitor understood that racial and cultural stereotypes are dehumanizing.

These responses are encouraging, for they tell us that the museum visitor is ready to learn. We can also see, however, that they are searching for connections to culture, belief, and expression, not necessarily to history. Many museum visitors are seeking a positive, deeply reflective experience, with indigenous cultures as a way of learning about themselves.

Otis Tufton Mason, the Smithsonian's first curator of the Department of Ethnology, stated that one task of an anthropologist was the universal search for the "secrets of man's origins, progress, and destiny."[3] No doubt there was some genuine interest in seeing what could be learned from indigenous cultures. The prevailing racism and cultural myopia of the late nineteenth century, however, only seemed to perpetuate backward ideas about inclusion.

The Columbian Exposition of 1893 was a festival of many tribes presenting their cultures and performing a variety of actions, from dancing to battle reenactments. It was full of Indian processions, villages, and Disney-like landscapes. The Columbian Exposition presented Indians and Inuit people as "life-group" dioramas, frozen in a timeless past. The diorama captured an elemental aspect of survival in a pristine environment. It was like a living painting of the past made "real" in three dimensions. The reconstructed Indian villages allowed the visitor to get a sense of what the old lifestyle was like, and the Indian performers sang, danced, made bows and arrows, posed for photographs, and earned a few dollars. These representations gave the viewer an impression that they were actually watching Indians at work or play.

Today we still see the same kind of format used by museums. Contemporary Indians explain their history, perform tribal dances, and generally entertain us with their culture. While the words have changed, and our perception of indigenous culture has certainly improved, the basic museological approach has remained the same. The only real difference is that we make considerably more money at this kind of interpretation. Was the 1893 Indian Congress, full of brightly decorated Native Americans reenacting cultural activities and historical dramas, a Native place? I think not. It was a totally artificial view of staged cultures, despite the involvement of Indian curators and Indian presenters.

Ironically, it was a Tuscarora chief from my own community who helped arrange the Indian displays at the Columbian Exposition. In 1891, Cornelius C. Cusick (1835–1904) was appointed honorary and special assistant in the Department of American Archaeology and Ethnology of the World's Columbian Exposition. Cusick had served as a lieutenant in the Union Army and also fought against Crazy Horse, Red Cloud, and Sitting Bull in the Dakota Territory. Archaeology was his hobby, and Cusick was credited with the discovery of the petrified remains of an ichthyosaurus at Fort Randall, South Dakota, in 1873. He also spent much time investigating the ancient Indian mounds in Ohio. Cusick began to collect American Indian objects for the displays that took place in Chicago. Less than twenty years later, he was creating museum displays to commemorate the very people he used to hunt down.

If we look at Cusick as a Native curator, we could say that the 1893 Indian Congress was the first example of "giving voice" to indigenous perspectives. While that sounds politically correct, it is ludicrous. His curatorial work was instrumental in the world's perception of Indians, yet we have to question the bias that he may have overlaid on the representation of Indians. Simply being an Indian is not enough to suggest that he would represent an insider's view of Native culture. His story represents the diversity of ways in which Indians actually lived in that era. Despite my indictment of early museums, dioramas, and expositions, many Indian professionals actually shaped these formats of representation.

Ideas Over Objects

The NMAI is premised upon a new approach. The opening exhibitions were to be driven by ideas rather than objects. There would not be a regional approach such as that used by the Columbian Exposition. Instead, broad themes would be used to group the stories. Objects would be used to illustrate those stories. In addition, the use of indigenous selectors would be employed to make the presentations more authentic. Actually, this was not as new an idea as we may believe. During the Columbian Exposition, the International Congress of Anthropology held a conference with the theme "Men, Not Things." The field itself was questioning previous approaches to material culture and began to look at how environments, beliefs, mythologies, and social organization shaped culture.

Despite the emphasis on ideas and story, the NMAI still relies upon objects to engage the visitor. Some art historians feel that art manifests the order of human thought, as well as the intensity and strength of our emotions or beliefs. Through art we can pass on a shared experience. This is a powerful role for art objects. Museums use this idea effectively, allowing visitors to draw their own feelings and conclusions by contemplating a work of art. This means that, despite the issues of context, we should not deny the inherent ability of the object to transport the viewer to different planes of consciousness. The art of Allan Houser and George Morrison was presented along these lines at the NMAI. While there was brief biographical and historic context, viewers were allowed to spend as much time as needed to derive their own power from the art. It is a contemplative process that defines art museums and many indigenous places. This aspect seems to refute my previous arguments, yet that is also the nature of the modern visual arts—to make objects for this type of gazing.

Think of petroglyphs. They have existed in their places for many years. Each generation of indigenous people visits those places to refresh its collective memory of the meaning of the images. Some you don't recognize. Some have affinity with contemporary practice. Contemplation of the meaning is enhanced by the place, the surrounding environment, and the fact that you are standing at the same place that countless ancestors have also stood. You are there because they were once there. It is the kind of connection to place that is hard to replicate in museums. Removing the petroglyph and transporting it to the museum, or recreating it on fake museum rocks, removes it from its familial relationship. While the museological petroglyph might refer to the actual context, it cannot perform the function of that context. The museum visitor cannot leave a mark (without getting arrested!).

Non-Indigenous Visitor Expectations

In 1993, the National Museum of the American Indian conducted a survey of its 70,000 members. The responses (summarized below) inform us about what these museum patrons wanted to see in the new museum. About 93 percent of the members believed the museum should focus on both ideas and objects, rather than just one or the other. One-quarter wanted to see the exhibits organized by "tribal nation" rather than theme, region, topic, historic period, or current issues. This points out the need for a familiar frame of reference.

When asked what type of exhibition techniques they would like the museum to employ, 53 percent of the members did not want to see high-tech video and computer exhibitions, preferring instead recreated environments, live demonstrations, hands-on, interactive exhibitions, and written materials. This seems to recall the Indian Congress approach. Surprisingly, 74 percent wanted the museum to discuss topics of current social concern, such as health issues and economic problems on reservations.

When asked what Native American values inspired the members' interest, 85 percent believed the environmental values of Indian society have the most relevance in today's world. This was followed by spiritual values (77 percent), respect for the elderly (72 percent), family relationships (68 percent), tribal governance and traditions (51 percent), and organic agricultural practices (49 percent). This is an interesting contrast to the views of nineteenth-century anthropologists who held that Indians were in a savage state of human cultural development.

In 1893, the public was interested in "modern" Indians. A contemporary article entitled "Indians at the Exposition" provides some sweeping generalizations about Indians of that era, and makes for a telling contrast with the interests expressed by members of the NMAI:

> Some of them are as wild and uncivilized as they were a century ago, while others are found fairly well educated. . . . Some are farmers, other stock raisers, while a few find employment working trades learned while attending the reservation of the government schools in their boyhood days. . . . The women do most of the work, the men, excepting the Pueblos, regarding manual labor as somewhat degrading. . . . The Indian man may not be lazy, but as a rule he has not learned to work . . . it might be said that the average Indian is a very social individual and is fond of company.

This represents another form of cultural diplomacy—that of using negative reinforcement in the social engineering of Native Americans.

Museums have a difficult time wrestling with how to present contemporary issues in their exhibitions and programs. Such issues often spawn highly emotional reactions in both indigenous and non-indigenous constituents. There is seldom a dominant indigenous opinion or voice on some matters. Patrons and donors of the museum often object to the issues. Tribal museums are also caught in an interesting dilemma. Since most are sanctioned and funded by the tribe, tribal politics intrude. It is difficult to raise sensitive or controversial topics in the local museum. Often our own communities have a very narrow view of what a museum is supposed to do. Tribal museums are supposed to be places of pride that celebrate the goodness of the culture. This can create a situation in which we can be in denial about our own history and the state of our own societies. In this regard, the tribal museum becomes the best practitioner of cultural diplomacy.

White-Out of Red Stains

One area where I felt the NMAI dropped the ball was in dealing with history. I do not mean that there should have been a diatribe on genocide and broken treaties. Instead, I felt the museum could have done more to help the visitor understand the major turning points of history, the major trends and issues that affect our lives today. While the video introduction to the history section set up a great premise, the exhibitions did not seem to deliver on that idea. I wanted to know more. I wanted more to think about. I wanted to be challenged more. Instead, I saw too many Bibles, too many guns, and too much gold stripped of its identity. While this is one major theme in European history, our history runs deeper than that. As an artist, this could have made for an interesting installation—the impact of gold, guns, and God upon indigenous peoples. The reality and humanity of the impacts, however, were missing for me.

There is a general dislike in museums for examining the difficult eras of genocide. Murder, rape, and suicide do not make good subjects for family consumption. The challenge for a museum is to find new ways to talk about difficult topics without turning off the visitor or upsetting the sponsor to the point where censorship takes place. It is a delicate balance. Most Native historians do not want the public to feel guilty about the past, but we do want them to understand the causes for the tragic events and the ongoing consequences of those events. Sometimes those are not nice pictures to look at. An indigenous space would not shy away from this task. It is place where the wounds of the past are still healing. It is a place where we need to talk about those wounds in order to heal. We, as indigenous people, keep our history alive in our hearts and minds. We can recall events as if they took place just yesterday. An indigenous place is alive with stories of all kinds—some that force us to tears, others that make us laugh. Stories are about emotions. We can animate history in a way that was missing from the NMAI. Emotionless history is boring.

This gets to why I hate museums. Actually, I hate the ideas that gave birth to museums. To me, museums created an intergenerational wound, one that lives within us and is not easily forgotten. The desecration of Indian graves and the theft from the dead have resulted in a serious violation of our human rights. It is a process of dehumanization that has allowed the museum field to consider human remains as archaeological resources, sacred objects as specimens, and our cultural patrimony as intellectual property.

There is another Native-born theory called "ethnostress" that purports to explain our current dysfunctional state as the result of self-hatred, born from generations of being told that our culture is worthless. According to the authors of this theory, "ethnostress" creates an overwhelming sense of fear, anger, and powerlessness in indigenous people. "Ethnostress" leads to confusion about religion, education, sexism, racism, economic issues, and child rearing. This in turn causes a disruption of personal and group identity and upsets our joyful experiences on the journey of life. In addition, anthropology painted Indians as being acculturated and less-than-worthy because they did not live up to the image of the diorama-Indians created by anthropologists. This produced generations of Native Americans who felt like strangers in their own homeland.

When my parents were born, they were considered wards of the government. They were not citizens and did not have the same rights to redress the wrongs done to them and their relatives. Being a second-class person carries its own baggage. My grandparents had to deal with boarding schools, and they all chose to have their children speak English in order to protect them from the racism and prejudice faced by previous generations. There is no doubt that our people became dazed and confused.

We have become a people suffering from a kind of Stockholm syndrome. We have fallen in love with our captors. We adopt their ways. We support their goals. Museums have become a natural arena for us to perform within. We have spent millions and millions trying to find our place with the museum, yet we never seem to arrive. Intense, relevant, and vibrant explorations in history are needed, not official or apologetic history—just an opportunity for indigenous communities to engage in their own discussion about how history reveals both opportunities and threats to indigenous nationhood.

Museums and Nation Building

There is a physiological role for museums in connecting people to larger cultural ideas and informing them on the significance of place, family, and community. This might explain why so many Native Americans showed up to march in the procession to open the new museum. The emotions and energy of thousands of indigenous people cannot be denied. It was people marching with their feet to say, "We do matter." Regardless of what the exhibitions say, many indigenous people felt the museum represented an overdue sign of respect and a political act of reconciliation. Perhaps this is part of the healing that needs to take place; this is the conclusion of cultural diplomacy.

The physiological role is also why tribal museums are important. They can help our wounded relatives recover their identity and sense of purpose. They can promote healing, rebuild connections, and most importantly, welcome people back home to their place of origin. Tribal museums and cultural centers can help rebuild pride and dignity as well as encourage a sense of responsibility to revitalize tribal language and arts programs—and they can help return repatriated items back to the cultural and spiritual practitioners of the community. They can do all of this if they remain community focused and not become visitor centers catering to the needs of tourists. Indigenous nation-building and museums can encompass five key elements:

Cultural role: How can the museum generate cultural expression, which in turn will unite and empower the indigenous community as it begins to better manage its own cultural patrimony? The museum does not determine what culture is; it only facilitates the indigenous nation's explorations in such matters.

Social role: How can the museum become a power site to promote enlightened understandings of the diversity and uniqueness of indigenous societies while it enhances cross-cultural communications? The museum can create a new sense of place and opportunity as it provides validation for indigenous social protocols.

Economic role: How can the museum foster a real sense of prestige and standing for indigenous nations in the world community? While this can be tied to tourism, the museum can have a role in creating cultural resource-management capacity and professional development of indigenous scholars, curators, administrators, and presenters.

Psychological role: How can the museum help foster a sense of destiny by learning from the past to help healing and wellness in indigenous societies? The museum can bring people into contact with ideas, beliefs, and practices of larger significance, thereby providing both a real connection to the past and a feeling of stability in facing the future.

Language role: How can the museum give voice to indigenous societies? The museum can bring people together through song, story, language, and indigenous literature. Only by expressing itself as an indigenous people will indigenous culture survive.

To accomplish these kinds of goals, the NMAI has to add a radical dimension to its programming. Instead of looking at indigenous people as suppliers of culture or as consultants to the museum-driven agenda, there must be a new partnership with the indigenous nation, one that is predicated on the museum supplying the support services for community-based culture, language, and art initiatives.

If we accept the premise put forth by Native speakers that individual tribal cultures can only be understood through their own Native languages, then it is imperative that museums work with indigenous communities to assure that our unique languages not only survive but also thrive. When assessing the state of our indigenous societies, we first have to understand the health of our languages and the linguistic practices necessary to teach indigenous languages as a second language. In many ways, the federal government and the reformers of the nineteenth century got their wish. They wanted all Indians to think in and speak English. While we still have some older folks who are fluent in their Native languages, the languages that sustained our people for countless generations are on the verge of becoming silent. It is true that non-indigenous linguists have studied and recorded many of the languages, yet much of their work remains inaccessible to the communities. Much is written in outdated or incomprehensible linguistics.

The National Museum of the American Indian could be the place where indigenous linguists come to study and learn ways to teach tribal languages, working with the new strategies of education that museums have developed. The visual resources of the museum could be a great asset to tribal language programs. The archival information at the NMAI and other federal repositories could gain new life in the hands of indigenous educators. The NMAI needs a research agenda that sets in motion its programs, priorities, and collaborations for the next few decades. Language, history, and art should be the main parts of that agenda.

The 1990 mission statement of the NMAI talks about the museum's role in enhancing "the development, maintenance, and perpetuation of Native culture and community." It is a bit lofty and presumptuous. Perpetuation of the community is a political act as much as it is a cultural or educational one. The museum cannot help the nations maintain their sovereignty in the ever-increasing legalistic world. It can, however, help indigenous communities understand the historical context of the shifting sands of sovereignty, and it can help indigenous communities gain insight into the social landscape whereby such issues are resolved.

If we accept the "ethnostress" notion of intergenerational dysfunction, then we have to do more than show pretty objects in well-designed displays. The responsibility of keeping indigenous societies from imploding is well beyond the capacity of the NMAI, and perhaps any museum. The NMAI and other major museums, however, can do more to help build the community infrastructure needed for transitions away from dysfunctions and the negative legacy of racism. The museums can also help train a new breed of Indian professionals and intellectuals who are deeply ingrained in their community. By providing logistical and practical support, the NMAI can make its notion of "the fourth museum" a reality.

NOTES

1. Brian Wallis, "Selling Nations: International Exhibitions and Cultural Diplomacy," in Daniel Sherman and Irit Rogoff, eds. *Museum Culture: Histories, Discourse and Spectacles* (Minneapolis: University of Minnesota Press, 1994).

2. All relevant quotes are from Mark Bennitt, *The Pan-American Exposition and How To See It* (1901).

3. Otis T. Mason, *What Is Anthropology?* (Washington, D.C., 1883).

Bells worn by traditional dancers in India. Gift from Amareswar Galla to W. Richard West, Jr., September 20, 2004. Photo by Katherine Fogden (Mohawk).

AMARESWAR GALLA

Director, Sustainable Heritage Development Programs
Research School of Pacific and Asian Studies
The Australian National University

On Being Indian:
Museums and Indigenous Engagement
in Human Development

Vandanam, Vanakkam, Namaste, Namaskaram. Greetings from South India, the place where I was born, brought up, and educated.

My professional life during the last three decades has been informed by the struggle of indigenous people on all five continents to reclaim their ability to represent themselves, celebrate their identities, and develop their sense of self-esteem. My central concern is the location of heritage and health in well-being.

Although my life began in a remote part of India, where I spent my early days like a frog in a well, my current position as a professor at a major university, as vice president of the International Council of Museums in Paris, and as the UNESCO technical adviser on the location of culture in development, gives me a strong moral and professional responsibility to raise some key concerns regarding museums and indigenous people. In celebrating this historical occasion of the affirmation of the indigenous peoples of the Western Hemisphere, I would also like you to consider some of the challenges ahead of us.

As we celebrate, we should remember the multiple journeys out of anger, violence, alcohol, drugs—all those negative forces that so many indigenous people experience as subaltern populations, where power is in the hands of the "other." Young people in indigenous communities everywhere continue to struggle with the balancing act of growing up between indigenous and non-indigenous discourses of culture and well-being. Let me share with you the story of a young indigenous man and his grandmother, a woman who helped him turn his life around.

The young man was in prison, and was allowed only one meal each day. His grandmother would bring his meal and serve it on a banana leaf. There was no electricity, so she carried with her an earthen oil lamp with a wick. She was often angry with him. She said, "Look at that lamp, how it burns itself out. Now look at yourself. You're wasting your youth, and you're useless. You're burning yourself out, too. But look again at this lamp: while it burns, at least it gives some light."

His grandmother gradually transformed his life, helping him become a person who would constructively engage in dealing with indigenous issues. She drew on the conventional wisdom and authority of her people. How could the negative energy that consumes so many young indigenous people be turned around into a positive force for change? How could we use the forces of globalization to voice indigenous concerns and improve the quality of life for indigenous people?

Without addressing as a priority the well-being of indigenous communities, the paradigm of the "noble savage in the Garden of Eden" will only be reinvented. Select indigenous people, with participation facilitated by dominant groups, will become tokens, performing to the tune of the marketplace, "ecotourism," and indigenous cultural tourism. What role can museums play so that the forces of globalism do not compromise the integrity and innate values of indigenous cultures.

That said, tell me this: What's an Indian doing at the opening of an American Indian museum?

India: An Case for Institutional Change

In 1500 BC, the *Rig Veda*, the first of the great Sanskrit texts, mentions the indigenous people of India. They are described as dark-skinned; we know all the negative images that come with that. By the third century BC, Ashoka, the Mauryan emperor, united the whole of the Asian subcontinent. Ashoka is thought to be one of the most progressive and exemplary leaders in the history of the world, and his edicts, engraved on rocks and pillars throughout that vast region, espouse nonviolence and tolerance. Having conquered ruthlessly the last of the frontiers in peninsular India, the Kalinga kingdom, and in remorse over the devastation caused by his exploits, this great Emperor lay down his arms and shifted from *Dig Vijaya* (conquest by force) to *Dharma Vijaya* (victory through right actions and peaceful engagement). He introduced Buddhism to most of South Asia and beyond. His legacy continued for a long while, with Buddhism as the world's largest faith, until the Cultural Revolution in China in the last century.

Buddhism brought with it a reconciliatory and respectful approach towards indigenous cultures. Historical studies of India often emphasize the cultural role of Brahmins and Hindus in societal formations, and freely use such expressions as "Sanskritization" and "acculturation." Theories of assimilation of "small traditions" of indigenous societies by the "great tradition" rarely acknowledge the indigenous societies whose rootedness in the subcontinent was critical to the evolution of India's rich cultural diversity. I urge you to consider the large number of museums and art galleries in the United States and elsewhere that have amassed major collections of Buddhist art and material culture. The majority of these cultural warehouses perpetuate the Orientalist discourse of Western art and aesthetics, rarely addressing the origins, cultural context, or contextual societal formations that informed the growth and spread of Buddhism. My argument is that, in addressing indigeneity in museums, we should engage critically the colonial typification of indigeneity through the anthropological lens. It is often forgotten that His Holiness the Dalai Lama is the spiritual leader of an indigenous people, the Tibetans. To understand and engage with the diversity of indigeneity at a global level, we must continue to interrogate the construction of the category in museums.

In present-day India, seven percent of the population is indigenous. Very few museum professionals are aware of the fact that the majority of indigenous people in the world live in India and China. In the former, they are constitutionally designated and were acknowledged as early as 1950. Jawaharlal Nehru, the first prime minister, made a commitment to such concepts as "affirmative action" and "positive discrimination" regarding indigenous people. Before any other country, India developed an affirmative action program. In pursuing this objective, as well as the gross under-representation of indigenous people in Indian cultural infrastructure, a major national museum for tribal people was established in Bhopal, India: the Indira Gandhi Rashtriya Manava Sangrahalaya.

The complexity of India's indigenous peoples has produced legacies that have ranged from assimilationist approaches to ones of displacement and dispossession in pre-colonial, colonial, and post-colonial times. The edicts of King Ashoka are witness to the recognition of indigenous people as *atavikas*. Historically, rulers have made alliances with indigenous people through power relations articulated through exchanges of prestige goods and matrimonial alliances. Where I come from in the south Indian state of Andhra Pradesh, the *Ikshvaku* kings, at the turn of the first millennium AD, became devout Buddhists. One of the earliest Ashokan *stupas* is at Amaravati, although the substantial part of the sculptures and encasing is the centerpiece of the Buddhist Gallery in the British Museum. Scholars now acknowledge that Nagarjuna, the propounder of Mahayana Buddhism, was born in Amaravati and that he lived there and in Vijayapuri, or Nagarjunakonda, for most of his life. His Holiness the Dalai Lama is sponsoring a *kalachakra* ceremony in January 2006 at Amaravati. Studies of *Ikshvaku* material culture have shown that it was highly likely that they were the present-day tribal people known as the Chenchus. Yet, no reference is ever made to the aboriginal people of the area in either the British Museum or the several museums in India. It is as if an object-centered museology, informed by a sophisticated contemporary reinvention of the Orientalism in the West, had failed to recognize the original inhabitants, whose dexterous carving skills produced some of the most significant early sculptures of Buddhism in the great museums of the world.

Indigenous Communities and Museums: Breaking the Cycle
The relationship between heritage, health, and well-being is rarely understood despite the call for locating culture in integrated local area planning and sustainable development by the World Commission for Culture and De-

velopment and the Stockholm Action Plan on Cultural Policies in Development. While the need to take a holistic approach is applicable to all populations irrespective of cultural borders, the situation of the world's indigenous peoples, often in vulnerable positions because of the impacts of historical legacies, requires particular attention. The Cultural Diversity Policy of the International Council of Museums emphasizes this point.

Contemporary indigenous communities face a number of challenges in addressing their sense of place and identity in a rapidly globalizing world. The challenges include the legacies of colonization, displacement, and dispossession, which lead to a loss of access to land and hence a loss of economic and spiritual wellness; intergenerational loss of heritage consciousness; the breakdown of cultural discipline; and the erosion of cultural self-esteem. The resultant hopelessness, the breakdown of health and well-being, and the growth of internal violence—sometimes self-directed violence—are common. Young people incarcerated in prisons are sometimes found dead in custody. There is also domestic violence as well as violence within and between communities. Alcohol, substance abuse, and the use of so-called recreational drugs pose enormous problems.

These problems are faced by indigenous people here in North America, in India, in Australia, and in Belize. It doesn't matter where you go. In reflecting on these truths, I ask you: What is the role of museums in civic engagement? Can the National Museum of the American Indian (the NMAI) provide leadership? If you could celebrate the achievements on the Smithsonian Mall, with the Capitol only a stone's throw from the museum, how does and how should the NMAI engage with indigenous communities in the Western Hemisphere and perhaps around the world?

I cannot help thinking of the inspiration that I have been fortunate to have from the U'mista Cultural Centre in Alert Bay, Canada. Gloria Cranmer Webster, the curator, said that the purpose of their programs is for "our young people to know who they are and to feel good about themselves. If they feel good about themselves and believe that they are worthwhile people, they'll be something in the world." By addressing the erosion of cultural self-esteem, museums and living heritage centers can play a critical role in indigenous community renewal, community consolidation, and the ability of communities to participate in a diversified mainstream.

Moving Beyond Photo Opportunities

Indigenous people continue to be prisoners of stereotypes. In the mid-1990s, I was in the Philippines for the Asia Pacific Regional Assembly of the International Council of Museums. My hosts took me to a large shopping mall that had just opened in Manila. The mall was featuring a big promotion for Lego, the children's toy company. I walked into a surreal scene, with people dressed for an Old West reenactment as part of the promotion. Suddenly there was silence. I had long, plaited hair in those days. Two "cowboys" approached me, took off their hats, and said, "We would like a photo with you." They had me sit next to a very beautiful "Native American" woman, and then they put their guns against my head for the photograph.

Let's deconstruct this a little. People from a country that had been forcibly taken by the United States were pretending to be a slightly different version of their own great-grandparents' oppressors. Half the world away from the original scene, these people became cowboys, and I, a darker person from yet a different part of the world (but one that had also been brought up in a former colonial country), was suddenly playing their Indian. It reminded me of an exhibition from the Woodland Cultural Centre, in Brantford, Ontario, entitled "Fluffs and Feathers," which dealt with stereotypes of the "Indian" in the imagination of the West. Being, or trying to be, an "Indian" can be very complicated and challenging, especially if you want to do something more than act as a prop for photographs. One of the challenges for museums is to deal with the continuing stereotyping of indigenous people across the world, some derived through local histories and others through shared colonial legacies.

An Indigenous, Migrant Experience

My first job as a migrant in Australia in 1985 was supported by the National Aboriginal Education Committee and the Aboriginal and Torres Strait Islander Advisory Committee to the Council of the National Museum of

Australia. At that time, there were only two Aboriginal people employed as professional staff on the payroll of Australian museums, galleries, libraries, archives, national parks, and world heritage areas. This is out of a total of more than 14,000 employees across Australia. There were several others on what was then called the Community Employment Scheme, a dole-for-work plan, which did more damage than good to people's self-esteem.

Tourism has remained the fastest growth industry in Australia, as is true elsewhere in the world, and the cultures and the heritage landscapes of the Aboriginal people and Torres Strait Islanders provide a significant part of the marketed cultural experiences for visitors. Yet community benefits to the primary stakeholders from the consumption of these experiences are controlled mainly by the majority. My job was to develop a national affirmative action program that would address this imbalance.

This was a challenge because it caused a considerable amount of consternation among establishment leaders. They were used to clear delineations, to "us" and "them," to the kind of binary that comes with always saying "Aboriginal" Australia and "Aboriginal" research. But I was ideologically neither white nor black, as far as they were concerned, and before we could even begin work, it created problems. Some scholars and professionals objected that I was educated in India and that I was not Australian, but I was under the guidance of an Aboriginal and Torres Strait Islander committee. They said, "But that's exactly why we brought him, so that we can get away from this 'us and them' situation and bring about change." Finally, the establishment grew reconciled to the fact that I was an alien by saying officially, "It's okay, he belongs to the third ethnicity." We had only one simple goal: the participation of indigenous people at every level and in all processes of heritage management. By this I mean the participation of indigenous people, not as token people, as people to be consulted, as people to be used for photo opportunities, but as people who participate and engage in the whole process of museology.

In Australia we worked toward a simple goal, but that does not make for a simple journey. When a survey was conducted in 1985, some heritage institutions said, "We'd like to employ Aboriginal people, but they'd go walkabout." We also heard, "Aboriginal people don't want to work in museums. Why are you trying to make them work in museums?" One eminent scholar even tried to persuade us that the students and cadets whom we had already recruited should really be enrolled in majoring in "prehistory." The fact that indigenous people want to participate in heritage management was difficult to accept for many people not all that long ago. We drew participants nationally through a cadetship program and directly negotiated with museums, galleries, national parks and world heritage areas for placements. In this way, placements were negotiated in partnership with the institutions.

In the years that followed, experiences in Australia were further enriched with interventions and lessons learned in other parts of the world. A workshop to draft a Code of Ethics for the Caribbean Museums Association in Belize highlighted its own complexities. The population of Belize—which includes the Garifuna, descendants of Carib people; Africans who had escaped from slavery; the Maya, tribal people from Belize; and the descendants of various colonial transplanted populations—was a multicultural mix that posed complex questions for museums to address. Afro-Caribbean participants objected to the use of the term "indigenous," arguing that they did not come to the Americas applying for jobs and that the new discourse of indigeneity marginalizes them once again. It was emphasized that the Afro-Caribbean question lies at the core of reconciling the cultural rights of indigenous people in Central America. This is an issue in Jamaica as well. However, I was told that Jamaicans don't say they are Afro-Caribbean, or Arawak. They don't say they are indigenous or Indian. They are Jamaican and that's it.

Colonialism did its work in Central America and the Caribbean, just as it did in other places of the world, and this still significantly affects people today. How do we deal with these histories? How do we engage with these communities and constructively handle the problems that are derived from their histories? When we talk about cultural rights and human development, *these* are the issues that become critical for museums.

From 1994 to 1999, I spent several months working on the review and restructuring of apartheid institutions in South Africa. It was the biggest project of my life, and something very interesting happened. Almost everyone, especially the international community, assumed that "Black" means "indigenous." They forgot the Khoi, the Nama, the San—the aboriginal peoples of South Africa. However, Nelson Mandela—or Madiba, as he was affectionately called by his tribal name—made a personal effort to make sure land repatriation and the rights of the indigenous people of South Africa were addressed as a priority.

The question everybody asks is: Who is indigenous to Africa? By the most basic of arguments, according to recent DNA research, almost all of humanity outside Africa descends from just a few mothers. Who is indigenous in Africa is a big issue, a big debate. Narrowing this down quite a bit, we may ask: How do we deal with indigenousness in museums in Africa?

And on to Asia. China has the world's largest indigenous population, numbering more than one hundred million people, most of whom are referred to as ethnic minorities. They have a minister who deals with indigenous issues who is himself indigenous. Members of the bureaucracy are indigenous, mostly located in the western provinces, but their work in the administration is based in Beijing. One of the world's largest museums for indigenous people is in Beijing. They are building another to compete with it.

There are a number of indigenous community cultural centers and eco-museums in China. In Hanoi, there is the Vietnam Museum of Ethnology, which mainly addresses indigenous peoples. The national priorities include economic development for indigenous peoples, once again referred to as ethnic minorities. The National Commission for Culture and the Arts in the Philippines has a separate policy category for indigenous people. These policies are just the beginning of an effort to address the well-being of indigenous people in Asia. In the adjacent Pacific there is another consideration beyond cultural policies: In about twenty years' time, we will not have two Pacific Island countries, because they will be under water as a result of global warming. Where do their indigenous people go?

It doesn't matter where you travel—across Asia, throughout the world—there are questions about the survival of indigenous/tribal people. And everywhere we turn within those communities, we see the whole vicious cycle of colonization, displacement, and dispossession. Do museums have a role to play? This is a question that we must ask ourselves constantly.

The NMAI's Leadership to the World

What can the NMAI in particular do for indigenous people around the world? There are three things. Let me first say that this museum is a great achievement. It is the beginning of a global dialogue. I know it focuses on the Western Hemisphere, but other people in the world want to participate in the dialogue, too, and learn from it. I have often stated that the global discourse about museums and indigenous people is largely centered on Canada, the United States, Australia, and New Zealand. These countries dominate international discourse in museology concerning indigeneity, but the world is very culturally diverse. Indigenous cultures are significant in this diversity. Where are the diverse perspectives? How can we build on the achievements of these four countries?

The majority of indigenous peoples don't have resources to attend conferences, meetings, and workshops. They did not have the resources to come to the sessions of the Working Group on the World's Indigenous Populations in Geneva. Participation was often moderated by agencies and governments that have different priorities and approaches to indigeneity. There is a responsibility here for the brothers and sisters in these four countries to remember the diverse voices when they engage in these dialogues.

Each indigenous community is unique. Each has its own histories and issues to grapple with. In this way, we have much in common. I have discussed some of the negative things that bind us together, but we can share triumphs as well as troubles. I can never forget how the *Te Maori* exhibition gave indigenous people a sense of pride. Some indigenous people saw only the exhibition catalogues in libraries, but it made them feel proud of their cultures and of what they have achieved. We *need* to be proud of these things.

One of the continued challenges for the NMAI is the kind of museology we see here, the shift that is occurring within the framework of our typically post-colonial situations. What's happening in museums in these four countries—Canada, the United States, Australia, and New Zealand—does not happen so much elsewhere. The NMAI could help facilitate the diversity of indigenous discourse in museums around the world, from the Western Hemisphere and beyond. That's the first thing the NMAI can do. Provide moral and professional leadership.

The second thing the NMAI could do to help internationally is very straightforward. In November 1999, we brought together in a workshop in Cairns, Australia, museum and cultural center directors from various Pacific Island countries together with Aboriginal and Torres Strait Islander curators. One of the main issues was the definition of a museum, and how the conventional definition is not really relevant to the indigenous people of Pacific Island countries. We made a recommendation that the International Council of Museums needed to revise their definition of a museum, and it has been. We need people to ensure that this kind of engagement is constructive, meaningful, and has the voices of indigenous people embedded in it. The NMAI has a very important responsibility in this process of transforming museological development.

Lastly, the United Nations Development Program recently released its Human Development Report. For the first time, the U.N. recognized that cultural freedoms and cultural rights are an important part of human development. This is significant. If we want to break away from the vicious cycle mentioned earlier, we need accountability in the way indigenous peoples' issues are addressed within the context of human development. The NMAI can and should be a part of this process, too. Perhaps, the NMAI could facilitate a global dialogue for the establishment of indigenous cultural indicators in human development

I want to finish with another anecdote. Last year as a member of the Program Committee of the American Association of Museums, I was in New Orleans for the Program Committee meeting. I was early, so after having a shower, I went down into the street quite oblivious of the significance of the neighborhood. I found myself on Bourbon Street in the French Quarter of New Orleans, and I discovered all these wonderful jazz places. It was fantastic. I had a great time, but I have never been photographed so much in my entire life. Everywhere people were stopping me and saying, "Excuse me, could we have a photo with you?" And I was asked again and again, "Are you a *real Indian?*" This is happening now, in the United States.

How do we break from this silent, two-dimensional role as a photo opportunity to the image of Indians in all their complexity? The "imagined" Indian. The "real" Indian. How do we examine indigenousness and cultural diversity from the perspective of indigenous people? These are some of the challenges. The journey has just begun. An old Chinese saying mentions that a journey of a thousand miles begins with the first step. The project is without an end. The NMAI could light the long road to the cultural freedom of indigenous peoples. Meanwhile, I remain sincerely yours—a real "Indian"—professionally, spiritually, and emotionally grateful for this opportunity to speak here.

BLESSING: *Ganonyok*

We have come here to our gathering place and have exchanged greetings with one another. We have found old friends and made new. We have offered words of thanksgiving for the well-being of all the people who journeyed here and have arrived safely. We put our minds together now as one and offer these thoughts to the Creator, that now our minds are one as we give thanks for the people.

And next we turn our thoughts to the earth—that our mother, the earth, is continuing to sustain all life, doing her job according to the way the Creator intended at the beginning of time. She is still working to the benefit of all living things, and so now we put our minds together, turn our thoughts to the Creator, and give thanks for our mother, the earth.

And next we turn our thoughts to the waters that flow beneath the earth, that flow upon the back of the earth, and that stand here as ponds, as lakes, as great bodies of salt water. Each and every one of the living things in them are doing their job according to the way the Creator intended, and so we put our minds together now as one and give thanks for the waters.

And next we turn our thoughts to the plants that the Creator has provided; they are medicines. The very small ones that grow next to the earth, they're the bushes and the shrubs. Each and every one of them has a role to play in continuing life, interrupting those small illnesses that may set the people, the animals, or the birds aside. So at this time we give thanks and acknowledge all of those medicine plants, and now our minds are one.

And we give thanks for the foods that sustain us, and turn our thoughts to the Creator and offer words of thanksgiving, and our minds are one.

And next we turn our thoughts to the four-leggeds running along the edge of the woods, both the small and the large ones. They have sustained all life here on earth and give up their lives for our well-being. So at this time we give thanks to the Creator for the four-leggeds, and now our minds are one.

And next we acknowledge the birds flying overhead. Those birds have a role to play as our teachers. We hear their songs in the morning and we are beautified in our world by their colors and their feathers. At this time we acknowledge and give thanks for those birds, and now our minds are one.

And next we turn our thoughts to the many types of trees—the trees that bring forth medicine for our people, the trees that warm our homes, the trees that made the elements of this particular building. And so we give thanks for all of those trees, and turn our thoughts to the Creator and now our minds are one.

And next we acknowledge that the wind, most of the time, is a benefit to human beings and to all living things. But we also know that the wind is strong enough to scrape things right off the face of the earth. So at this time we give our thoughts to the four directions of the winds and to the Creator, and now our minds are one.

And next we turn our thoughts to the thunder beings, which announce that new water is coming in the form of rain to replenish the springs and the wells and to nourish all living things here on the earth. So we put our minds together now as one and give thanks for the thunder beings, for the lightning, and for the new water, and now our minds are one.

And next we turn our thoughts to the sun, our elder brother. He makes his journey across the sky each and every day, traveling from east to west, providing the light of the day and doing his job just the way the Creator intended at beginning of time. And so now our thoughts are turned to him, and we give thanks, and now our minds are one.

And next we also mention that our grandmother, the moon, continues to look after that cycle that women have, which allows them to bring forth life into this world, thereby connecting our grandmother moon with the children as well as with the women. We turn our thoughts now to this and we give thanks, and now our minds are one. And arrayed about our grandmother are the stars, and these stars have a role to play, too. We use them for setting our ceremonies. In the past, we used them for finding our way, if we got lost at night. During the hottest days of the summer, the stars provide moisture to the plants. So we turn our thoughts now to the stars, put our thoughts together as one, and now our minds are one.

And next we acknowledge the four messengers who look after each and every one of us, and who have their hands upon our shoulders as we travel. They continue to do their job, and we give thanks to them at this time. May they have peace and we as well, and now our minds are one.

And next we turn our thoughts to those teachers, those messengers, who have come to all the different people with the same message: to love one another, to treat one another with respect, to treat all living things with respect. We should listen to these instructions that the Creator has provided us through these messengers. And so we turn our thoughts to these great teachers, and we put our minds together as one, and now our minds are one.

And next we acknowledge that everything I have mentioned is the Creator's hand that we see. And so, as one of those who is a faith keeper within my tradition, I gather your thoughts together to say this great, great, good *thank you* to the Creator on behalf of each and every one of you—giving thanks for this day, for this gathering, for this place that we are in, and for the goodness and the love of our children and all those who are coming in the future.

Doneh ho. (These are my words).

—*This blessing was offered by G. Peter Jemison (Seneca) at the conclusion of the Opening International Symposium at the National Museum of the American Indian, on September 20, 2004. Members of the Six Nations Haudenosaunee (also known as the Iroquois Confederacy) offer the blessing on social and ceremonial occasions.*

View of the landscape and water feature at the National Museum of the American Indian, Washington, D.C. Photo by Maxwell MacKenzie, © 2005.

CONTRIBUTORS

W. RICHARD WEST, JR., founding director of the National Museum of the American Indian, Smithsonian Institution, is a member of the Cheyenne and Arapaho Tribes of Oklahoma. In 2002, he was made a Peace Chief of the Southern Cheyenne.

ELAINE HEUMANN GURIAN is a senior museum consultant and founding deputy director for Public Program Planning at the National Museum of the American Indian, Smithsonian Institution.

JETTE SANDAHL is director of the Museum of World Culture in Gothenburg, Sweden. Previously, she was director of exhibitions and public programs at the National Museum of Denmark.

GEORGE F. MACDONALD is director emeritus of the Canadian Museum of Civilization. The author of more than 150 publications, Dr. MacDonald has written extensively about the Native cultures of the Pacific Northwest, the changing role of museums in a global context, and issues ranging from repatriation of Native artifacts to information technology in museums.

BERNICE L. MURPHY is vice president of the International Council of Museums (ICOM-Paris). She was founding assistant director and chief curator, and later director of the Museum of Contemporary Art in Sydney, Australia.

DAME CHERYLL SOTHERAN is director of Creative Industries at New Zealand Trade and Enterprise. She was the founding director of the National Museum of New Zealand Te Papa Tongarewa, and has chaired the New Zealand Art Gallery Directors' Council and the Art Galleries and Museums Association of New Zealand.

DES GRIFFIN is the Gerard Krefft Memorial Fellow at the Australian Museum, in Sydney, Australia. He retired in September 1998 after twenty-two years as director of the museum. Dr. Griffin was appointed a Member of the Order of Australia (AM) in 1990 in recognition of services to museums.

RICHARD W. HILL SR. currently serves as a guest lecturer at the Six Nations Polytechnic in Ohsweken, Ontario, and the Tekarihwake Program in the Language Studies Department at Mohawk College, in Hamilton, Ontario. A member of the Beaver Clan of the Tuscarora Nation, he was former assistant director for Public Programs at the National Museum of the American Indian, Smithsonian Institution.

AMARESWAR GALLA is the director of Sustainable Heritage Development Programs in the Research School of Pacific and Asian Studies at the Australian National University, Canberra.

GUIDE TO FURTHER READING

The Changing Presentation of the American Indian (Washington, D.C.: National Museum of the American Indian, Smithsonian Institution, in association with University of Washington Press, Seattle, WA, 2000).

Fred R. Myers, *Painting Culture: The Making of an Aboriginal High Art* (Durham and London: Duke University Press, 2002).

Gerald McMaster and Clifford Trafzer, eds. *Native Universe: Voices of Indian America* (Washington, D.C.: National Museum of the American Indian, Smithsonian Institution, in association with National Geographic Books, 2004)

Bernice Murphy and Djon Mundine, eds. *The Native Born: Objects and Representations from Ramingining* (Sydney: Museum of Contemporary Art, 2000).

Lawrence E. Sullivan and Alison Edwards, eds. *Stewards of the Sacred* (Washington, D.C.: American Association of Museums, in cooperation with the Center for the Study of World Religions, Harvard University, 2004).

Duane Blue Spruce, ed. *Spirit of a Native Place: Building the National Museum of the American Indian* (Washington, D.C.: National Museum of the American Indian, Smithsonian Institution, in association with National Geographic Books, 2004)

Tom Hill and Richard W. Hill Sr., eds. *Creation's Journey: Native American Identity and Belief* (Washington, D.C., and London: Smithsonian Institution Press, 1994.

Ivan Karp and Steven Lavine, eds. *Exhibiting Cultures: The Poetics and Politics of Museum Display* (Washington, D.C.: Smithsonian Institution Press, 1991).

Index